SINS

The Poison of
the Heart

r Haifaa Younis

KUBE
PUBLISHING

Jannah
Institute

Sins: The Poison of the Heart

First published in England by

Kube Publishing Ltd,
Markfield Conference Centre,
Ratby Lane Markfield,
Leicestershire LE67 9SY,
United Kingdom.

Distributed by

Kube Publishing Ltd.
Tel: +44(0)1530 249230
email: info@kubepublishing.com
www.kubepublishing.com

All royalty proceeds from the sale of this book go to Jannah Institute.

Cataloguing-in-Publication Data is available from the British library

ISBN 978-1-84774-215-5 Paperback
ISBN 978-1-84774-216-2 ebook

Cover design: Afreen Fazil (Jaryah Studios)
Typesetting: LiteBook Prepress Services
Printed in: Elma Basim Turkey

Dedication

To the two gems who taught me everything. I am the result of their hard work and dedication.

My parents

Wa-qul Rabbi irhamhuma kama rabbayani saghira

And Say: "Lord, show mercy to them as they nurtured me when I was small." (*al-Isrā*, 17:24)

Table of Contents

Preface   vii

Chapter 1   **The Importance of Learning About Sins**   1

Do Not Undermine Sins   4

Immorality   6

Self-Accountability   7

Lessons from the Prophets   8

Adam   8

Nuh   10

Salih   11

Lut   11

Musa   12

Chapter 2   **Major Sins: The Poison that Kills the Heart**   13

Identifying Major Sins   15

Chapter 3   **Sins Cause a Deficiency in Knowledge and Worship**   25

Deprivation of Knowledge   25

Deficiency in Worship   31

Protection   34

Chapter 4   **Sins Weaken our Relationship with Allah** ﷻ   **37**

Protection   43

Chapter 5   **Sins Strengthen our Relationship with
Shaytan**   **49**

The Tricks of Shaytan   54

Chapter 6   **Sins cause Affliction**   **63**

Sins withhold Provision   66

Sins cause Calamities   69

Protection   72

Chapter 7   **Sins affect the Heart**   **77**

Sickness of the Heart   82

Goodness of the Heart   86

The effects of Good and Bad Deeds on the
Heart   88

Protection   93

Index   97

Preface

In the name of Allah, the Most Merciful, the Most Compassionate.

All praise is for Allah 🕮. We praise Him 🕮, seek His 🕮 Help, and ask His 🕮 Forgiveness. We seek refuge in Him 🕮 from the evil of our own souls and from the wickedness of our deeds. Whoever Allah 🕮 guides, nothing can make him lost, and whoever He 🕮 makes lost, nothing can guide him. I bear witness that no one has the right to be worshipped but Allah 🕮, Who has no partner, and I bear witness that Muhammad ﷺ is His slave and His Messenger.

عَنْ أَنَسٍ، أَنَّ النَّبِيَّ صَلَّى اللهُ عَلَيْهِ وَسَلَّمَ قَالَ: كُلُّ بَنِي آدَمَ خَطَّاءٌ وَخَيْرُ الْخَطَّائِينَ التَّوَّابُونَ

'An Anasin anna al-nabiyya, salla Allahu 'alayhi wa-sallam qala: "Kullu Bani Adama khatta'un wa-khayru al-khatta'in al-tawwabun."

It was narrated from Anas that the Messenger of Allah 🕮 said: "Every son of Adam commits sin, and the best of those who commit sin are those who repent." (*Ibn Majah*, 4251)

We all sin (commit acts of disobedience to Allah 🕮) on a daily basis. However, in many cases, we are unaware and neglectful of the sins we commit, and underestimate the consequences they have on us, our relationship with Allah 🕮, other people, and even the environment.

We are often torn between the comfort of ayāt like:

قُلْ يَـٰعِبَادِىَ ٱلَّذِينَ أَسْرَفُواْ عَلَىٰٓ أَنفُسِهِمْ لَا تَقْنَطُواْ مِن رَّحْمَةِ ٱللَّهِ إِنَّ ٱللَّهَ يَغْفِرُ ٱلذُّنُوبَ جَمِيعًا إِنَّهُۥ هُوَ ٱلْغَفُورُ ٱلرَّحِيمُ ۝

Qul Ya-'ibadi al-ladhina asrafu 'ala anfusihim la-taqnatu min rahmati Allahi. Inna Allaha yaghfiru al-dhunuba jami'an. Innahu huwa al-tawwabu al-rahim.

Say: "O My servants who have transgressed against themselves [by sinning], do not despair of the Mercy of Allah. Indeed, Allah forgives all sins. Indeed, it is He who is the Forgiving, the Merciful."   (*al-Zumar* 39:53)

and the gravity of ayāt like:

وَٱعْلَمُوٓاْ أَنَّ ٱللَّهَ شَدِيدُ ٱلْعِقَابِ ۝

Wa'lamu anna Allaha shadidu al-'iqab.

"and know that Allah is severe in penalty."
(*al-Anfal* 8:25)

Questions that may cross our minds about sins include:

- – What price will I pay for them?
- – Will Allah 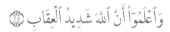 forgive me?
- – Will others be affected by my sins?
- – Are all sins the same?
- – Do all sins have consequences?

This book is a collection of lectures I delivered at the Jannah Institute's Tuesday Night Program series in collaboration with the Islamic Centre of Irvine (ICOI) from October to December 2022 about the nature, consequences, and remedies of sinning.

It contains seven chapters, beginning with the definition and understanding of the word 'sin' in the Qur'an and Hadith, the differences between major and minor sins, and the most common types of sins in Islam. It then goes on to discuss the importance of learning about sins; how sins weaken our relationship with Allah ﷻ, the *din* and our spiritual heart; and how they strengthen our relationship with our greatest enemy - Shaytan.

This book attempts to bridge the gap between the traditional work of our rich and powerful heritage of classical Islamic scholars and the reality of the intensive and busy contemporary times that we currently live in.

If you don't understand the concept of sins, this book is for you, both as a new Muslim or someone with a Muslim background who did not have a chance to learn much about this topic.

For those who have some knowledge but choose not to live by what they have learnt, this book can help you understand the concept of sins on a deeper level and will hopefully, God willing, serve as a motivation for you to pay greater attention to avoiding sins in your daily life.

If you are doing your best to avoid sins but still find yourself failing, this book can be a useful tool to learn some tips and tricks that can help you on your path to avoiding sins, getting closer to Allah ﷻ, and working for our ultimate purpose and goal in life - Jannah al-Firdaus.

The information compiled in this work has been based on classical Islamic resources, such as the Qur'an and Hadith. The translation of the Qur'an used in this book is *Saheeh International*, while the Hadith primarily comes from *Kutub al-Sittah* (six canonical collections of Hadith). To further deepen our understanding of this topic, I also consulted books of *tazkiyah* by some of the classical authors, such as Imam Ibn Al-Qayyim, Ibn Al-Jawzi, Abu Talib Al-Makki, and others.

May Allah ﷻ accept this deed as a *sadaqah jariyah* that will benefit us and the generations that come after. May Allah ﷻ guide us to the straight path, keep our hearts strong and steadfast on it, grant us the strength to avoid sins, and bestow upon us His ﷻ Mercy, Forgiveness, and Pleasure.

Dr. Shaykha Haifaa Younis,

April 9, 2023 / Ramadan 18, 1444, Makkah, Saudi Arabia

Chapter 1

The Importance of Learning About Sins

The topic of sin is something to be learned in more detail by every Muslim. It is paramount that we delve into the details of what sins are and what they mean for us as servants of Allah ﷻ.

Abdullah ibn al-Mubarak, may Allah ﷻ be pleased with him, very eloquently described sins in a short poem:

وَيَتْبَعُهَا الذُّلَّ إِدْمَانُهَا   رَأَيْتُ الذُّنُوبَ تُمِيتُ الْقُلُوبَ

وَخَيْرٌ لِنَفْسِكَ عِصْيَانُهَا   وَتَرَكُ الذُّنُوبِ حَيَاةُ الْقُلُوبِ

I came to know that sins kill the heart,
Once I become addicted, I become humiliated
When you stay away from sins, your heart will come alive
The best thing you can do for yourself is to go against your *nafs*.

Here, he reminds us that our spiritual hearts need to be alive. It isn't enough for them to be beating and keeping us physically alive; we must ensure that we are acting in obedience to Allah ﷻ and don't involve ourselves in sin.

But what exactly is a sin? In the Arabic language, sin is referred to as ذنب (*dhanb*) – something that is wrong, immoral or a crime.

1

For example, *dhanb* is used in the Qur'an when Allah ﷻ commands the Prophet Musa (*'alayhi al-salām*) to go to Pharaoh and convey the message, to which Prophet Musa replied:

$$\text{وَلَهُمْ عَلَىَّ ذَنْبٌ فَأَخَافُ أَن يَقْتُلُونِ ﴿١٤﴾}$$

Walahum 'alayya dhanbun fa-akhafu an yaqtulun.

"And they have a **crime** against me, so I fear they may kill me." (*al-Shuʿarāʾ*, 26: 14)

The same word is also used by Allah ﷻ in *Surah al-Takwir* (ayah 8-9) where the ignorant custom of killing young girls is referred to:

$$\text{وَإِذَا ٱلْمَوْءُۥدَةُ سُبِلَتْ ﴿٨﴾ بِأَىِّ ذَنۢبٍ قُتِلَتْ ﴿٩﴾}$$

Wa-idha'l-ma'udatu su'ilat bi-ayyi dhanbin qutilat.

"And when the baby girl buried alive, is asked for what crime she was killed."

Allah ﷻ will ask the killers on the Day of Judgement what crime or sin the young girls committed to have been killed so ruthlessly.

One of the greatest Companions and Caliphs, Umar ibn al-Khattab, may Allah ﷻ be pleased with him, buried his daughter alive before he accepted Islam. People saw him crying when these verses were recited and asked him if he was missing his daughter, to which he replied: "When I was burying her, she was removing the dust from my beard." Unfortunately, burying girls was the norm, but Qur'anic revelation put an end to this custom by declaring it a sin.

In addition to the above definitions of sin as a crime, a sin can also be understood as:

- Any disobedience to Allah ﷻ that Allah ﷻ has forbidden, whether it is major or minor.

- Any action that Allah ﷻ has deemed punishable in the Qur'an.
- Any action or offence that goes against moral or religious law.
- Any wrongful action or fault committed against a human being. If we commit a sin against another person, it is by default disobedience towards Allah ﷻ.

We may think that it isn't very important to learn about sins because they have become so common, and we all inevitably commit them. However, it is vital that we understand that sins don't just affect our Hereafter, they also affect the present and our life in this world. Committing sins can affect our home (family and children), the community we live in, the *ummah* and even the Earth itself. We may see the effects immediately, we may see them after some time has passed, or we may not see them at all during our lifetime, but our children and future generations may see the impact of those sins after we have passed away.

Imam Ahmad reported on the authority of Wahb: "The Lord said in His Revelations to the Children of Israel, 'When I am obeyed, I am pleased. When I am pleased, I bestow My Blessing and there is no end to it. When I am disobeyed, I am Angry. And when I am Angry (with My servant), I curse him, and My curse reaches his seventh child (generation).'"

As we can see from the above narration, sins have lasting effects and are not to be taken lightly. Take for example, not waking up for Fajr, which is a major sin. We may not see any immediate effects, and we will continue with our lives as normal. He ﷻ doesn't punish us straightaway, as we are given the chance to fix our ways. However, the sins do not disappear until and unless we repent sincerely and completely with the intention to never repeat it.

An extremely important point to remember about sins is that they will affect our heart. Gradually, over time, our spiritual heart will become sick and die if we repeatedly sin. A clear sign of this is when we no longer feel any remorse for our sins, and it may even get to a point where we enjoy committing them. We may also witness others openly disobeying Allah and ignore it or try to justify their disobedience, rather than speaking out. We may even, God forbid, no longer be conscious of the fact that these people are disobeying Allah . These are major signs that our hearts are sick and dying, if not already dead.

Do Not Undermine Sins

Imam Ahmad made a very profound statement in which he said: "Do not look at the smallness or insignificance of a sin but look at the one you have disobeyed." This statement should be enough to make us stop in our tracks and change our perspective on the matter of sinning. Sins are not something that we can just wave off as insignificant because they are ultimately disobedience to our Creator, Allah .

When we don't perform *salah*, we are disobeying Allah just as Shaytan did. We make excuses for not performing *salah*, and no excuse is acceptable except that which has been specifically mentioned. For example, women who are menstruating cannot perform *salah* and those who are not of sound mind are exempt.

Imam Ahmad said: "Abd al-Rahman ibn Jubayr ibn Nafir, who narrated from his father, said: 'When Cyprus was conquered, families were separated (those who embraced Islam from those who did not), and left crying due to their separation. I saw Abu'l-Darda' weeping on his own and asked him: 'O Abu'l-Darda', what makes you cry on a day when Allah has made Islam and its people victorious?' He replied: 'Woe unto you O Jubayr! How worthless are people in the sight of Allah after they rejected His command, when once they were a sovereign nation. They turned away from the command of Allah , so this was their fate.'"

Abu'l-Darda' didn't see it as an outright victory because he saw that people who had so much power were separated from each other because they disobeyed Allah .

Imam Ibn al-Qayyim said: "The reason I don't sin is not because I am pious, but because Allah ﷻ is protecting me. And the moment I start sinning, Allah ﷻ will have removed the protection from me and allowed it to happen." We know that Allah ﷻ is All-Merciful and All-Forgiving, but He is also capable of removing His protection from us and allowing us to do whatever we want. Whenever we sin, it has nothing to do with other people or Shaytan, but it shows the state of our relationship with Allah ﷻ and the fact that we have been behaving in a way that has led us to disobedience.

Umm Salamah narrated: "I heard the Messenger of Allah ﷺ saying: 'When sins spread amongst my *ummah*, Allah ﷻ will set His punishment upon them.' I asked: 'O Messenger of Allah ﷺ! Would there not be among them some pious people at that time?' He replied: 'Yes, there would be.' I said: 'So, what will Allah ﷻ do with such people (the pious ones)?' He replied: 'They will suffer the punishment, like the other people, but then they would benefit from the mercy of Allah ﷻ.'" (*Ahmad*)

What can we understand from the above narration? We are currently witnessing sins spreading amongst our *ummah* like wildfire, and there is no denying this fact. When a punishment comes, we are all at risk of suffering, but this should not stop us from trying to become the best Muslims that we can be. We should all strive to be from the most righteous so that Allah ﷻ may have mercy on us and save us.

Al-Hasan al-Basri said: "This *ummah* will stay under the protection of Allah ﷻ as long as its scholars do not support its leaders, and its pious people do not vindicate the condition of its wrongdoers, and its righteous people do not disregard its evil people. But if they do that, Allah ﷻ will remove His assistance from them, and set against them oppressive regimes to afflict them with a horrible torment."

If we think about ourselves, how many of us get upset if someone treats us badly or speaks to us in a way that we don't like? Yet, if we see someone else committing wrong or being wronged, we say it's none of our business. We disregard the sinful behaviour of others and choose not to take any action and, unfortunately, don't realise that in doing so we become involved in such behaviour, along with the wrongdoers.

Sins will always have consequences. They will affect our hearts, our homes, our communities and even our mental health. We must ask Allah ﷻ for forgiveness, and we must make the intention to fix our ways and ask Allah ﷻ to guide us towards obeying Him and the Messenger ﷺ.

Immorality

We can see that as immorality (fornication) has increased in societies around the world, new illnesses and diseases have also emerged. Immorality is not to be taken lightly as it has lasting, negative effects on society.

Abdullah ibn Umar narrated: "The Messenger of Allah ﷺ turned to us and said: 'O *muhajirun* (migrants), there are five things with which you will be tested, and I seek refuge with Allah ﷻ lest you live to see them. Immorality does not appear among a people to such an extent that they commit it openly except that plagues and diseases that were never known among the predecessors will spread among them. When they do not weigh and measure with justice, they will be stricken with famine, severe calamity, and the oppression of their rulers. When they withhold *zakat*, rain will be withheld from the sky, and if it were not for the animals, no rain would ever fall on them. They break their covenant with Allah ﷻ and His Messenger, and so Allah ﷻ will enable their enemies to overpower them and take some of what is in their hands. Unless their leaders rule according to the Book of Allah and seek all good from that which Allah has revealed, Allah ﷻ will cause them to fight one another.'" (*Sunan Ibn Majah*, 4019)

Ibn Abi'l-Dunya also reported that Anas ibn Malik said: "I went with another man to see A'ishah, and he asked her: 'O Mother of the believers, tell us about the earthquake?' She said: 'When they authorise fornication, drinking of wine, the use of musical instruments, Allah ﷻ commands the earth: 'Tremble with them so that they might give up and repent.' Otherwise, He ﷻ would destroy it upon them.' The man asked: 'O Mother of the believers, is it a punishment for them?' She replied: 'Rather it is some advice and mercy for the believers, but a punishment and curse for the disbelievers.'"

Anas then said: 'I have never heard a Hadith after the death of the Messenger of Allah ﷺ which made me happier than this Hadith.'

Self-Accountability

It's also important to understand that we will never be able to change if we blame someone or something else for our disobedience to Allah ﷻ. We cannot keep blaming Shaytan for making us disobey Allah ﷻ because, ultimately, we have been given the free will to choose our actions. When it's Ramadan and all the *shayatin* are chained up, we have nobody to blame but ourselves for going against what Allah ﷻ has ordered.

Sufyan al-Thawri once said: "I commit a sin and I see a result of it in the behaviour of my wife, servant and animal." When we commit sins, their effects trickle into the lives of those around us. When we do something wrong, we will see the result of it. If we want to avoid this, we must analyse our own behaviour and actions and take the right steps to change ourselves for the better and to not disobey Allah ﷻ. If we wake up in the morning and find that our car isn't starting, we look for the reason it isn't starting, and the same should be done for our actions as Muslims.

An important lesson that we can learn from *tazkiyah*, is that we should think about how we may have wronged Allah ﷻ. If a person is rude to us, rather than saying that they are impolite, we must think about our actions that may have led to Allah 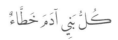 allowing that person to commit injustice on us.

There are many examples of how loving the *dunya* also is a sin, such as loving and preferring our sleep over waking up for *salah*, giving importance to our beauty and not dressing appropriately, loving and thinking highly of ourselves such that we talk badly about others and attack them, and loving money so much that we use any method to gain more of it. The *dunya* means children and wealth, and love for the *dunya* will not go away or change until we change ourselves.

Becoming deaf and blind to the guidance of Allah could mean that we hear a verse from the Qur'an but it doesn't affect us in any way. We could hear a Hadith of the Prophet Muhammad yet remain unbothered. We could even listen to an Islamic lecture or attend the mosque during Ramadan but remain unchanged because of the state of our heart. We need to look at our hearts, the way we are living our life and how we keep relations with others and with Allah. The law of this earth consists of cause and effect, and it is vital that we analyse ourselves.

Lessons from the Prophets

Adam

Nobody is immune to committing sins, as the Prophet Muhammad said:

$$كُلُّ بَنِي آدَمَ خَطَّاءٌ$$

Kullu bani Adama khatta'un.

"All the children of Adam commit sins."

However, although nobody is safe from committing sins, we must remember the way we deal with our sins and the effort we put in to seek Allah's ﷻ forgiveness.

In the story of Prophet Adam, may Allah ﷻ be pleased with him, we find that what caused him and his wife to be expelled from Jannah was their disobedience of Allah ﷻ. Adam, may Allah ﷻ be pleased with him, was forbidden by Allah ﷻ from going near a certain tree and eating from it. However, Shaytan continuously tempted him by beautifying a wrong action. Shaytan told Adam that if he ate from the tree, he would stay in Jannah forever, becoming immortal.

Allah ﷻ describes this in the following verse:

مَا نَهَىٰكُمَا رَبُّكُمَا عَنْ هَٰذِهِ ٱلشَّجَرَةِ إِلَّآ أَن تَكُونَا مَلَكَيْنِ
أَوْ تَكُونَا مِنَ ٱلْخَٰلِدِينَ ﴿٢٠﴾

Ma nahakuma rabbukuma 'an hadhihi'l-shajarati illa an takunaa malakayni aw takuna mina'l-khalidin.

"Your Lord has forbidden this tree to you only to prevent you from becoming angels or immortals." (*al-A'rāf*, 7:20)

Shaytan himself was also expelled from Jannah due to his disobedience, although he once had a lofty rank among the creations of Allah ﷻ. Following his pride and arrogance, Shaytan refused to prostrate to Adam (may Allah ﷻ be pleased with him), thus refusing the command of Allah ﷻ , as is described in the following verses:

قَالَ يَٰٓإِبْلِيسُ مَا لَكَ أَلَّا تَكُونَ مَعَ ٱلسَّٰجِدِينَ ﴿٣٢﴾ قَالَ لَمْ أَكُن
لِّأَسْجُدَ لِبَشَرٍ خَلَقْتَهُۥ مِن صَلْصَٰلٍ مِّنْ حَمَإٍ مَّسْنُونٍ ﴿٣٣﴾ قَالَ فَٱخْرُجْ
مِنْهَا فَإِنَّكَ رَجِيمٌ ﴿٣٤﴾ وَإِنَّ عَلَيْكَ ٱللَّعْنَةَ إِلَىٰ يَوْمِ ٱلدِّينِ ﴿٣٥﴾

Qala ya Iblisu malaka alla takuna ma'al-sajidin. Qala lam akun li-asjuda libasharin khalaqtahu min salsalin min

hama'in masnun. Qala fa'khruj minha fa-innaka rajim.
Wa-inna 'alayka'l-la'nata ila yawmi'l-din.

"Allah ﷻ said: 'O Iblis, what is the matter with you that you are not with those who prostrate?' He said: 'Never would I prostrate to a human whom You created out of clay from an altered black mud.' Allah ﷻ said: 'Then get out of it, for indeed, you are expelled. And indeed, upon you is the curse until the Day of Recompense.'"   (*al-Hijr*, 15:32-35)

Nuh ﷺ

فَكَذَّبُوهُ فَأَنجَيْنَٰهُ وَٱلَّذِينَ مَعَهُۥ فِى ٱلْفُلْكِ وَأَغْرَقْنَا ٱلَّذِينَ كَذَّبُواْ بِـَٔايَٰتِنَآ إِنَّهُمْ كَانُواْ قَوْمًا عَمِينَ ۝

Fakadhdhabuhu fa'anjaynahu wa'l-ladhina maahu fi'l-fulki wa-aghraqna'l-ladhina kadhdhabu bi-ayatina innahum kanu qawman 'amin.

"But they denied him, so We saved him and those who were with him on the ship. And We drowned those who denied Our signs. Indeed, they were a blind people."   (*al-A'rāf*, 7: 64)

The people of Nuh, may Allah ﷻ be pleased with him, were called to believe in Allah ﷻ and the last day, but they repeatedly rejected the message and were punished with a huge flood that drowned them. Allah ﷻ has mentioned to us in the Qur'an the punishments He sent down on previous nations; their arrogance, rejection and disobedience led to their downfall, as we learn from the following verses:

كَذَّبَتْ عَادٌ فَكَيْفَ كَانَ عَذَابِى وَنُذُرِ ۝ إِنَّآ أَرْسَلْنَا عَلَيْهِمْ رِيحًا صَرْصَرًا فِى يَوْمِ نَحْسٍ مُّسْتَمِرٍّ ۝ تَنزِعُ ٱلنَّاسَ كَأَنَّهُمْ أَعْجَازُ نَخْلٍ مُّنقَعِرٍ ۝ فَكَيْفَ كَانَ عَذَابِى وَنُذُرِ ۝

Kadhdhabat 'adun fakayfa kana 'adhabi wa-nudhur. Inna arsalna 'alayhim rihan sarsaran fi yawmi nahsin mustamir. Tanziu'l-nasa ka-annahum a'ajazu nakhlin munqa'ir. Fakayfa kana 'adhabi wa-nudhur.

" 'Ad denied; and how severe were My punishment and warning. Indeed, We sent upon them a screaming wind on a day of continuous misfortune. Extracting the people as if they were trunks of palm trees uprooted. And how severe were My punishment and warning." (*al-Qamar*, 54:18-21)

Salih ﷺ

And regarding Thamud, the people of Salih:

إِنَّآ أَرْسَلْنَا عَلَيْهِمْ صَيْحَةً وَاحِدَةً فَكَانُوا۟ كَهَشِيمِ ٱلْمُحْتَظِرِ ۝

Inna arsalna 'alayhim sayhatan wahidatan fakanu ka-hashimi'l-muhtazir.

"Indeed, We sent upon them one blast from the sky, and they became like the dry twig fragments of fence-builders." (*al-Qamar*, 54:31)

Lut ﷺ

And regarding the nation of Lut, of whom many people were involved in homosexuality:

فَلَمَّا جَآءَ أَمْرُنَا جَعَلْنَا عَـٰلِيَهَا سَـٰفِلَهَا وَأَمْطَرْنَا عَلَيْهَا حِجَارَةً مِّن سِجِّيلٍ مَّنضُودٍ ۝

Fa-lamma ja'a amruna ja'alna 'aliyaha safilaha wa-amtarna 'alayha hijaratan min sijjilin mandudin

"So, when Our command came, We made the highest part of the city its lowest and rained upon them stones of layered hard clay."   (*Hud*, 11:82)

Musa

And regarding the Pharaoh at the time of Musa:

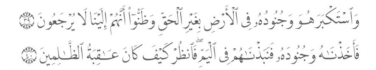

Wa'stakbara huwa wa-junuduhu fi'l-ardi bi-ghayri'l-haqqi wa-zannu annahum ilayna la yurja'un. Fa-akhadhnahu wa-junudahu fa-nabadhnahum fi'l-yammi fa'nzur kayfa kana 'aqibatu'l-zalimin.

"And he was arrogant, he and his soldiers, in the land without right, and they thought that they would not be returned to Us. So, We took him and his soldiers and threw them into the sea. So, see how was the end of the wrongdoers!" (*al-Qasas*, 28:39-40)

The Pharaoh went to the extent of saying: "I don't know any god other than me, and I am better than this useless little human being (describing Musa, peace be upon him)." We learn through the Qur'an that the punishments Allah sent upon people were similar, or befitting, to their sins. If we become arrogant, Allah will humiliate us. If we treat someone badly, we may also get treated badly.

Chapter 2

Major Sins: The Poison that Kills the Heart

What is a major sin? Simply put, a major sin is something that Allah ﷻ has told us not to do. If Allah ﷻ has forbidden an action in the Qur'an or through the Sunnah, it is classed as a major sin. A few examples of major sins mentioned in the Qur'an are as follows:

- "لا تقتلوا النفس"
  "Do not take a human life [kill a person]" (*al-Isrā'*, 17: 33)
- "لا تأكلوا مال اليتيم"
  "Do not come near the wealth of an orphan"
  (*al-An'ām*, 6: 152)
- "لا تقربوا الزنا"
  "Do not go near adultery [or do any action that can lead to fornication]" (*al-Isrā'*, 17: 32)

Abu Hurayrah, may Allah ﷻ be pleased with him, narrated that the Prophet Muhammad ﷺ said: "The son of Adam has been destined his share of fornication, which he will inevitably acquire. The eyes fornicate by looking, the ears fornicate by listening, the tongue fornicates by speaking, the hand fornicates by hitting, the foot fornicates by stepping. The heart loves and wishes. The genitals prove or disprove of that."

Imam al-Qurtubi has also described major sins as those which have been mentioned in the Qur'an or Sunnah either by name or by mentioning a severe punishment, or those which have been agreed upon by scholarly consensus. One example of this is in the following verse from the Qur'an:

وَٱلَّذِينَ يَنقُضُونَ عَهْدَ ٱللَّهِ مِنۢ بَعْدِ مِيثَـٰقِهِۦ وَيَقْطَعُونَ مَآ أَمَرَ ٱللَّهُ بِهِۦٓ أَن

يُوصَلَ وَيُفْسِدُونَ فِى ٱلْأَرْضِ أُو۟لَـٰٓئِكَ لَهُمُ ٱللَّعْنَةُ وَلَهُمْ سُوٓءُ ٱلدَّارِ ۝

*Wa'l-ladhina yanquduna 'ahda'l-Lahi min ba'di mithaqihi
wa-yaqta'una ma amara'l-Lahu bihi an-yusala wa-yufsiduna
fi'l-ardi ula'ika lahum'l-la'natu walahum su'u'l-dar.*

"But those who break the covenant of Allah ﷻ after con-
tracting it and sever that which Allah ﷻ has ordered to
be joined and spread corruption on earth - **for them is the
curse, and they will have the worst home."**
(*al-Ra'd*, 13: 25)

The lessons we can take from this verse are that we should not be
involved in injustice, wasting food and drink, harming or destroying
the earth (this could include throwing rubbish in places other than
bins or killing plants and trees unnecessarily), and ruining relationships with each other. Being involved in such actions invokes the
curse of Allah ﷻ, and this is no small matter as it ultimately means
that we will not be receiving the mercy of Allah ﷻ.

Ibn Taymiyyah has further clarified major sins in his statement:
"Every sin in which the doer is warned that he will not enter Paradise, or even smell the fragrance of Paradise, or it was said that the
one who does it is not one of us or is a wrongdoer – all of these are
major sins."

Allah ﷻ also tells us the following in the Qur'an:

إِنَّ ٱلَّذِينَ يَشْتَرُونَ بِعَهْدِ ٱللَّهِ وَأَيْمَـٰنِهِمْ ثَمَنًا قَلِيلًا أُو۟لَـٰٓئِكَ لَا خَلَـٰقَ

*Inna'l-ladhina yashtaruna bi-'ahdi'l-Lahi wa-aymanihim
thamanan qalilan ula'ika la khalaqa lahum fi'l-akhirati wa-la
yukallimuhum'l-Llahu wa-la yanzuru ilayhim yawma'l-qiya-
mati wa- la yuzakkihim wa-lahum 'adhabun alim.*

"Indeed, those who exchange the covenant of Allah ﷻ and
their [own] oaths for a small price will have no share in the
Hereafter; and Allah ﷻ will not speak to them or look at
them on the Day of Resurrection, nor will He purify them;
and they will have a painful punishment." (*Al Imran*, 3: 77)

What can we learn from this powerful statement? Disobeying
Allah ﷻ will undoubtedly have severe consequences for us on the Day
of Judgement, and so we should try and make it easier for ourselves
to obey Allah ﷻ and make it difficult to disobey Him. The Prophet
Muhammad ﷺ used the wording 'stay away' to emphasise the importance of keeping away from situations that can lead us to sin. For
example, this can be as simple as keeping a distance from people you
know are likely to engage in backbiting or avoiding purchasing something on instalments because of *riba* (interest). When we stay away
from something that Allah ﷻ has told us to stay away from, it becomes easier to obey Him and to act in a way that is pleasing to Him.

Identifying Major Sins

One Hadith in which the Prophet Muhammad ﷺ uses 'stay away'
is narrated by Abu Hurayrah, may Allah ﷻ be pleased with him:

"The Prophet ﷺ said: 'Avoid the seven great destructive sins.' The
people asked: 'O Allah's Messenger, what are they?' He ﷺ replied:
'To join others in worship alongside Allah ﷻ, to practise sorcery, to

kill a life which Allah ﷻ has forbidden except for a just cause, to deal with *riba*, to eat up an orphan's wealth, fleeing from the battle-field at the time of fighting, and to accuse chaste women who are good believers.'" (*al-Bukhari*)

The sins mentioned above are described by the Prophet ﷺ not mere-ly as sins but as being sins that will destroy us. As such, it is para-mount that we understand the severity of these sins and the actions that can lead to, or are a part of, committing these sins.

The first and foremost destructive sin mentioned is *shirk* - associating something or someone with Allah ﷻ. The second is sorcery (*sihr*), which includes doing it yourself or getting someone else to do it on your behalf. This may be to destroy a marriage, someone's health, wealth, or for any other reason. The third is to kill a person without a just cause. A just cause falls into those few exceptions Allah ﷻ has permitted – for example, in battle or when we have to protect our-selves. The fourth destructive sin is to be involved in *riba*, whether taking it or giving it. Unfortunately, it has become very easy and common for people to be involved in transactions which include interest, but we should refrain from such purchases due to the fact that it is a major sin, and we should not use any excuses to try and justify it. The fifth destructive sin is to take or use the wealth of orphans unlawfully. Whether the orphan is related to us or not, any wealth that they have is unlawful for us to consume. The sixth is to run away from the battlefield; this is cowardly and not befitting of a Muslim. The seventh and the last destructive sin is to accuse a chaste woman of a dishonourable act without any evidence. Whilst it is a sin to be involved in fornication or haram relationships, it is also a big sin to accuse a believing woman of being unchaste when she would not even dare to think of doing such an action.

Another powerful Hadith in relation to major sins is narrated by Abdullah ibn Masud, may Allah ﷻ be pleased with him, who said: "A man asked Allah's Messenger ﷺ: 'What is the greatest sin in

Allah's ﷻ sight?' The Prophet ﷺ replied: 'That you should treat anything as equal to Allah ﷻ when He has created you.' The man asked: 'What next?' to which he replied: 'That you should kill your child for fear that he may eat along with you.' The man asked: 'What next?' to which he replied: 'That you should commit adultery with your neighbour's wife.'"

It can often be easy to overlook those actions that treat something else as equal to Allah ﷻ or give something more importance than Allah ﷻ. For example, we might miss or delay our *salah* on purpose because we are 'too busy' with something else, or we may choose not to wear hijab because we worry about what people will say or we believe it takes away from our beauty. In these cases, we are giving other things more importance than Allah ﷻ, but our priority should be to fulfil His Rights before anything else, always obeying and worshipping Him ﷻ. Ask yourself, how often do you prioritise other concerns and make excuses not to put Allah ﷻ first? We should make the intention never to do this again, otherwise we will surely be of the losers in the Hereafter.

Another major sin mentioned in this Hadith is to kill your child due to the fear of not having enough food. This doesn't just hold the literal meaning of the word 'kill,' but it also covers the concept of people who say that they cannot afford to feed another child and so they decide not to have more children. Saying such things implies that we do not fully believe that Allah ﷻ is al-Razzaq, the Provider, and it is us who give ourselves sustenance. However, we should put our trust in Allah ﷻ just as the birds and animals put their trust in Allah ﷻ to sustain them each day.

The action of committing adultery is also mentioned again as a major sin in this Hadith. Whilst unlawful relations have become extremely common in many societies around the world, we as Muslims cannot accept it as normal. It is not something to be taken lightly, and we must understand the seriousness of this sin.

Taysalah ibn Mayyas narrates:

"I was with the Kharijites (Najadites) when I committed wrong actions, which I supposed were major wrong actions. I spoke to Ibn Umar who asked what actions they were, and I replied that they were such-and-such. Ibn Umar then said: 'These are not major wrong actions. There are nine major wrong actions, and they are: associating others with Allah ﷻ, killing someone, desertion from the army when it is advancing, slandering a chaste woman, usury (*riba*), consuming an orphan's property, heresy in the mosque, scoffing, and causing one's parents to weep through disobedience.'

Ibn Umar then said to me: 'Do you wish to separate yourself from the Fire? Would you like to enter Paradise?' I replied: 'By Allah ﷻ, yes!' He asked: 'Are your parents still alive?' I replied: 'My mother is.' He said: 'By Allah ﷻ, if you speak gently to her and feed her, then you will enter the Garden as long as you avoid the major wrong actions.'" (*al-Adab al-Mufrad*)

In addition to the major sins mentioned in previous Hadiths, this narration mentions two further actions which I would like to explain in a bit more detail:

- Scoffing or making fun of other people. This can be through words that we utter, looks that we exchange with one another, or gestures we make. Unfortunately, these habits are very prevalent amongst the youth and result in bullying.
- Causing parents to cry due to disobedience or bad treatment of them. Unfortunately, this often occurs with elderly or sick parents. It is common for us to 'lose our cool' and become impatient with them, saying hurtful things, or not looking after them properly, which inevitably causes them to cry. It also often occurs with youth who may speak rudely to their parents or 'huff' at them, roll their eyes, or shout. Such harsh behaviour causes parents much pain and hardship.

Ibn Umar ended this narration with a very important point. He told Taysalah that speaking gently to his mother and feeding her would grant him Jannah, as long as he avoided the major sins. From this, we learn that:

- Speaking to our parents in a gentle manner will undoubtedly carry lots of rewards for us. The situation may, at times, be difficult, but if we fight the urge to respond with anger and speak kindly and respectfully, Allah ﷻ, the Most Merciful, will grant us entry to Jannah.
- Feeding our parents is a means to earn the eternal reward. This includes cooking for them or making them tea, water, fruits, or meals as well as physically putting morsels of food in their mouths (especially if they are old or too weak and ill to feed themselves).
- Just as Ibn Umar gave Taysalah hope that he can have his past sins forgiven, we too should not put a person down but rather give them hope for salvation.

Avoiding major wrong actions and taking care of our parents will ensure a positive outcome for us in the Hereafter. Once our parents pass away, we lose a great opportunity to do good; we can no longer sit with them, talk to them, feed them, or serve them. We may come across people who tell us not to worry about taking time out for our parents or even go as far as to suggest that they could be sent to care homes, but we should always keep in mind the importance of treating them well (in the way that Allah ﷻ has told us through the Qur'an and the Prophet Muhammad ﷺ through the Sunnah). We should also make *du'a* for those who tell us otherwise because if they knew the rank of parents, especially the mother, they would surely not discourage us from doing our duty. May Allah ﷻ forgive them and grant them understanding.

Imam al-Dhahabi compiled a list of seventy major sins, which I will mention below so as to give a clear indication of the actions that many of us – knowingly or unknowingly – may take part in or have done so in the past. Once we know what these major sins are, it's vital that we make the intention not to be involved in them again and take all the necessary precautions to follow this through.

The Seventy Major Sins:

1. *Shirk* – associating anything with Allah.
2. Killing someone unlawfully.
3. Practising magic (*sihr*) – either by yourself or through someone else.
4. Not praying – this can mean that someone doesn't offer *salah* purely due to laziness, but it can also mean that a person may not believe that *salah* is an obligation, or they may say "Allah doesn't need my *salah*".
5. Not paying *zakat* – we may pay other taxes regularly, but that does not excuse us from paying our due *zakat*. It is an obligation given to us from Allah, Who we must hold in a higher position than any government.
6. Not fasting during Ramadan without a valid excuse (such as due to illness, travelling, breastfeeding, pregnancy etc.)
7. Not performing hajj when we are able to. This could mean purposely delaying hajj so we can buy a house, or until our children finish university or get married.
8. Disrespecting our parents – saying "uff," or "ugh," to them and walking away. Showing them any kind of disrespect is not allowed.
9. Abandoning relations/relatives.
10. Fornication and adultery.
11. Homosexuality.
12. Interest (*riba*).
13. Wrongfully consuming the property or wealth of an orphan.
14. Lying about Allah and His Messenger.
15. Frequent lying in general.

16. Running away from the battlefield.
17. A leader deceiving his people and being unjust to them.
18. Pride and arrogance.
19. Showing off.
20. Falsely testifying as a witness.
21. Drinking alcohol.
22. Gambling.
23. Slandering chaste women.
24. Stealing from the spoils of war.
25. Stealing in general.
26. Highway robbery.
27. Taking a false oath.
28. Oppression – this can come in the form of something as simple as not treating your sibling well, or taking their belongings just because you are older, or it could be something as big as oppressing the poor in society by not allowing them access to basic needs.
29. Illegal gains.
30. Consuming wealth that is acquired unlawfully.
31. Committing suicide.
32. Judging unjustly.
33. Giving and accepting bribes.
34. Women imitating men or men imitating women.
35. Being a cuckold – a man whose wife is sexually unfaithful or is regarded as an object of derision.
36. Marrying a divorced woman for the purpose of making her lawful again for the first husband.
37. Not protecting oneself from urine.
38. Learning knowledge of the religion for the sake of gaining worldly praise and concealing the knowledge (or not sharing the knowledge for the benefit of others). An example of this could be memorising the Qur'an so that people can say you are a *hafiz* or *hafizah* or making your children memorise the Qur'an so that people can praise you for being the parent(s) of a *hafiz* or *hafizah*.

39. Betrayal of trust.
40. Recounting favours.
41. Denying Allah's 🕮 decree.
42. Listening to or eavesdropping on people's private conversations.
43. Carrying tales (*namimah*) – this means to repeat false or questionable stories about something that you have heard.
44. Cursing.
45. Breaking contracts.
46. Believing in or visiting fortune-tellers and astrologers (practices such as palm-reading, tarot card reading etc.). Only Allah 🕮 has the knowledge of the Unseen.
47. A woman's bad conduct towards her husband.
48. Making statues and pictures.
49. Wailing loudly, tearing clothes, hitting oneself or pulling one's hair when an affliction befalls.
50. Treating others unjustly.
51. Overbearing conduct towards the wife, the servant, the weak and the animals.
52. Offending one's neighbour.
53. Offending and abusing other Muslims.
54. Offending people and displaying an arrogant attitude towards them.
55. Trailing one's garment in pride.
56. Men wearing silk or gold.
57. A slave running away from his master.
58. Slaughtering an animal which has been dedicated to anyone or anything else other than Allah 🕮.
59. Knowingly ascribing one's paternity to a man other than one's real father.
60. Arguing and disputing violently.
61. Withholding excess water.
62. Giving short weight or measure (for example, selling something for the price of a certain weight, but purposely cheating in the weighing of it).

63. Feeling secure from Allah's ﷻ plan, assuming that you know better.
64. Offending Allah's ﷻ righteous friends/servants.
65. Not praying in congregation, but instead praying alone without an excuse.
66. Persistently missing Friday prayers without an excuse.
67. Usurping the rights of the heir through bequests.
68. Deceiving others and plotting evil.
69. Spying – this can mean spying for the enemy of the Muslims or even spying on your own family members. For example, taking someone's phone and looking through it without their permission. This also applies to parents spying on the phones of their children unless they made a contract or agreed upon it.
70. Cursing or insulting any of the Companions of the Prophet Muhammad ﷺ.

As we can see, there are many sins in this list that are commonly carried out, so it is our duty to educate ourselves on the major sins and avoid committing any more for the sake of our Hereafter.

I would like to end this chapter with a quote from Abu Talib al-Makki's book *Food of the Hearts*, which sums up the different major sins in a uniquely memorable fashion, associating each with their respective body part:

Major sins are seventeen:

– Four of them lie in the heart, and these are: associating others in worship with Allah ﷻ, insistence on committing a sinful deed, despondence of Allah's ﷻ mercy (saying that we or someone else won't be forgiven and won't enter Jannah) and feeling secure against Allah's ﷻ plan.
– Another four are associated with the tongue, and these are: false witness accounts, slandering chaste women, false oaths, and sorcery.

- Three of them are in the stomach: drinking alcohol, consuming an orphan's wealth and property, and devouring usury (*riba*).
- Two of them are in the private parts, and these are: adultery and homosexuality.
- Another two are in the hands, and these are: unlawful killing and theft.
- One is in the feet, and that is fleeing from the battlefield.
- And finally, one is throughout the whole body, which is being undutiful and disrespectful towards one's parents.

Chapter 3

Sins Cause a Deficiency in Knowledge and Worship

In this chapter, we will look at how sins can affect us as individuals by (1) hindering our ability to learn or gain beneficial knowledge and (2) negatively impacting our acts of worship.

Deprivation of Knowledge

When it comes to learning or gaining knowledge, we often over-look how important it is for us to learn about Allah ﷻ and His commandments for us. Even if it is just ten minutes per day, we should set aside and dedicate that time to increasing our knowledge of Allah ﷻ and Islam.

Abu Hurayrah, may Allah ﷻ be pleased with him, reported that the Messenger of Allah ﷺ said: "Allah ﷻ makes the way to Jannah easy for him who treads the path in search of knowledge." (*Muslim*)

Jannah isn't only attained through fasting, praying and charity, but also through seeking knowledge. This means that although we may not think much of it, attending talks or classes in the mosque is one of the easiest ways for us to become regular in seeking knowledge and thus is one of the paths to Jannah. If we don't attend these sessions, rather than making excuses for why we don't attend, we should ask ourselves if we are doing our best to obey Allah ﷻ or could it be because of a sin that Allah ﷻ has distanced us from seeking such knowledge.

Our first point of call is to analyse our performance, asking ourselves what we did wrong so that we can prevent it from happening again. There are many different avenues for us to seek and learn knowledge in these modern times, yet we don't make use of them. Allah ﷻ has blessed us with so many ways to learn, but we don't appreciate the value of them. Those of us who are born into Arabic-speaking households, do we truly understand the blessing of knowing the Arabic language? It is the language of the Qur'an, and it is the language of Jannah, but we are not utilising it properly – we don't put in the effort to even recite the Qur'an properly, let alone reading other books written in Arabic by major scholars. Do we ever think how we will answer to Allah ﷻ about not using this blessing? Those who don't know Arabic, how much efforts have we given to learn the language and benefit from understanding the messages of the Qur'an directly from the words of Allah ﷻ?

Sahl ibn Sa'd reported that the Messenger of Allah ﷺ said to Ali: "I swear on Allah ﷻ, it will be better for you that Allah ﷻ should give guidance to one man through you, than that you should acquire the red ones among the camels." (*Abu Dawud*, 3661)

Ali, may Allah ﷻ be pleased with him, was one of the most beloved and closest Companions of the Prophet ﷺ. He was also someone who was not as well-off financially as some of the other Companions. The Prophet ﷺ knew this and made it a point to say that it would be better for him that Allah ﷻ allows someone to be guided through him than for him to be able to acquire a herd of the most expensive red camels.

What lesson can we take from this? Spreading knowledge by sharing it verbally, or by going one step further and practicing that knowledge, making an example of it to others, is a wonderful way of giving *da'wah*, and Allah ﷻ will surely guide others through us. We don't need to have a vast amount of wealth, a PhD in Islamic Studies, or the ability to give lectures to people, but what we can do is share the knowledge of whatever we have learned.

Likewise, the opposite is also true. If the way we dress, talk, or behave is not pleasing to Allah ﷻ – especially if Allah ﷻ has put us in the public eye – and someone copies us or uses us as an example to follow, we have indeed suffered a great loss in the sight of Allah ﷻ.

Wasting the years Allah ﷻ has given us on this earth by neglecting the pursuit of Islamic knowledge will surely be a great loss for us. We will have no excuse when we face Allah ﷻ; He has provided everything for us, yet we choose not to utilise or value it, for example, not putting in the effort to relearn forgotten surahs or lessons taught to us through the Qur'an and Sunnah.

Knowledge is a light which Allah ﷻ instils in our hearts, but our sinful actions cause that light to become diminished. When Imam al-Shafi'i sat with Imam Malik at the age of nine, and recited to him, Imam Malik was very impressed with his intelligence and deep knowledge, and advised the young Imam al-Shafi'i with the following words: "My boy, I see that Allah ﷻ has filled your heart with light, so do not extinguish it with the darkness of sin."

Sins can take away beneficial knowledge from us, and they will, first and foremost, take away knowledge about the One we are disobeying. Drawing a parallel, we can find many examples in our lives where we intentionally refrain from doing something which is asked of us, and as a result, find that a distance between us and the one whose request we ignored has been created. For example, if someone invites us to their home, favours us with many things and makes a polite request for us to take off our shoes, yet we choose not to listen and keep our shoes on whenever we visit, they may eventually stop inviting us to their home. In this case, we would have nobody to blame but ourselves for the distance between us and that person.

Abu Hurayrah narrated that the Messenger of Allah ﷺ said: "Lo! Indeed, the world is cursed. What is in it is cursed, except for the remembrance of Allah ﷺ and all that is relevant to it, the knowledgeable person and the seeker of knowledge." (*Jami' al-Tirmidhi*, 2322)

Here, the Prophet ﷺ was explaining that the world is of no avail to us as it will end. The *dunya* has, and should have, no value to us because we will be leaving it all behind. The only good in this world (which will also be of benefit to us in the *akhirah*) is the remembrance of Allah ﷺ, the teacher or scholar and a student of knowledge. We can engage in the remembrance or *dhikr* of Allah ﷺ during our daily tasks, such as when we're driving or cooking, or when we are out walking and admire or praise Allah's ﷺ creation.

In terms of learning, we should ask ourselves how much time do we invest, or are we willing to invest, in seeking knowledge? When we compare the time spent for learning to the time we spend in the kitchen, or at work or on social media, the majority of us are spending very little time seeking beneficial knowledge. If we are able to dedicate just one hour or so every day to learn, then we are saving ourselves and our *dunya* from being cursed and instead doing something that will benefit us in the Hereafter.

Imam al-Shafi'i felt that his memorisation of the Qur'an had become weak, and said the following famous poem:

شكوت إلى وكيع سوء حفظي ، فأرشدني إلى ترك المعاصي

I complained to Waki' (my teacher) about the weakness of my memory, so he ordered me to abandon sins.

وقال اعلم بأن العلم نور، ونور الله لا يهدى لعاصي

And informed me that knowledge is light. And that the light of Allah 🕮 is not given to a sinner!

We are quick to assume or generalise that our memory or ability to memorise becomes weaker as we age, but we do not think that it may, in fact, be because of a sin or sins that we have committed – it could be because of something we have watched, said, texted, read or listened to.

If we want to learn in a way that ensures that knowledge stays with us, we must keep away from sins. Although there are many different opportunities and avenues for us to learn, we won't be able to hold on to knowledge if we do not give up sins – no matter how small they are.

Abu Musa reported that the Prophet 🕮 said: "Verily, the parable of the guidance and knowledge with which Allah 🕮 the Exalted has sent me is that of rain falling upon the earth. There is a good piece of land which receives the rainfall and as a result there is abundant growth of plants, then there is a land hard and barren which retains the water and the people benefit from it and they and their animals drink from it, then there is another land which is barren, and neither is water retained nor does any grass grow. The likeness of the first one is he who develops understanding of the religion of Allah 🕮 and he benefits from that with which Allah 🕮 sent me. The second is one who acquires knowledge of the religion and teaches others. The third is the one who does not pay attention to the message and thus he does not accept the guidance with which Allah 🕮 sent me." (*Muslim*, 2282)

What type of land are we in according to this parable given by the Messenger of Allah 🕮? How often do we open the Qur'an? Do we only open it when someone dies or during Ramadan? Do we seek knowledge and then teach our children and family that knowledge? We may be able to quote Hadiths or verses from the Qur'an, but are we behaving hypocritically by not practising what we preach?

$$\text{يَـٰٓأَيُّهَا ٱلَّذِينَ ءَامَنُوا۟ لِمَ تَقُولُونَ مَا لَا تَفْعَلُونَ ۝ كَبُرَ مَقْتًا عِندَ}$$

$$\text{ٱللَّهِ أَن تَقُولُوا۟ مَا لَا تَفْعَلُونَ ۝}$$

Ya ayyuha'l-ladhina amanu lima taquluna ma la taf'alun.
Kabura maqtan 'inda'l-Llahi an taqulu ma la taf'alun.

"O you who have believed, why do you say what you do not do? How despicable it is in the sight of Allah is that you say what you do not do!" (*al-Saf*, 61: 2-3)

Many children complain that their parents will often demand of them what they themselves do not do. For example, they ask them to be respectful to everyone but often disrespect people themselves or they ask them to not speak ill of people but regularly gossip, backbite or lie. We don't need to become scholars, but if Allah ﷻ has told us to do something, we must understand it and apply it to our lives until it becomes a habit. Al-Hasan al-Basri said in one of his letters: "When people show that they possess knowledge but waste that action (implementation of that knowledge) and express their love for each other while their hearts hate each other, and cut their ties of kinship, then they will be subjected to the curse of Allah ﷻ, who will make them deaf and blind (to His guidance)."

If we have knowledge of something but don't apply what we have learnt, we are wasting it and not providing benefit to ourselves or those around us. This is not limited to the scholars, but to all of us; our knowledge should benefit not only ourselves, but our families and the wider community.

May Allah ﷻ make us from those who when presented with knowledge, take it, learn from it, apply it and benefit others with it.

Deficiency in Worship

Sins can also cause a deficiency in worship within us. Al-Fudayl mentions praying at night, and one issue we often face when it comes to praying at night is the fear of losing out on sleep. However, we don't need to be up half the night praying, we could in fact wake up just a while before Fajr and pray two *rak'ahs* of *qiyam al-layl*. Many people wake up early to travel to work, school or university, so what stops us from waking up a bit earlier than usual to perform a deed that will not only benefit us in this life but also the Hereafter?

Nowadays, it is extremely common for us to be using our mobile phones before going to sleep. Granted, sometimes it may be that we are reviewing the Qur'an on our phones or doing some other good, like texting our parents or helping someone. However, unfortunately, most of the time, we are scrolling through social media or watching some form of entertainment late into the night, and we may then miss Fajr the following morning. How many of us link this deficiency in *salah* to what we watched or said before going to sleep the previous night?

Abu Sulayman al-Darani said: "No-one leaves praying in congregation but as a result of a sin!" (*Sifat al-Safwah*)

If we were always in the first row at the *masjid* for *salah* but we stopped attending, we should ask ourselves what could we have done to displease Allah ﷻ such that He removed us from the first row or the congregational prayer?

A young man came to al-Hasan al-Basri and said: "Night prayers (*qiyam al-layl*) make me tired and sick." Al-Hasan replied: "It is your sins which have chained you." Once again, we can see that sins stop us from performing righteous actions. A wise man was once asked: "What is health?" And he replied: "When one day passes and you have not committed a sin!"

We should make *du'a* for ourselves that Allah ﷻ makes us from those who do not sin. Sinning is very easy to fall into because sins are not only appealing and accessible, but most people are engaged in them (everyone else does it, so why not me?). Our *nafs* is attracted to sins, and Shaytan uses this to his advantage. Other people may also influence us through certain sins, such as backbiting, gossiping, lying, cheating, being wasteful, showing arrogance, mistreating parents, looking at or listening to haram etc.

Ibn al-Jawzi said: "Punishments for sins may not always be external, as one of the righteous men of the children of Israel said: 'O Allah ﷻ, how much I disobey You and yet You don't punish me?' It was said to them: 'How much do I punish you and you are not aware of it? Have I not deprived you of the joy of intimate conversation with Me?'"

This is applicable to us even today. For example, if or when *salah* becomes difficult for us, it may be because Allah ﷻ does not want us to come in front of Him. He ﷻ may be depriving us of the chance to have an intimate conversation with Him through *salah*. Do we stop to think about what sins we may have done for it to come to this?

When we are going through a difficult time in our lives, we 'make a deal' by saying to Allah ﷻ that if He eases this situation for us, we will become better in our actions. However, many a time it happens that Allah ﷻ does indeed take away the problem, but we carry on disobeying Him and then He keeps giving until He wishes to take it all away.

We may be disobeying Allah ﷻ publicly or privately, yet Allah ﷻ carries on giving us everything we desire until a point comes where everything is taken away from us – including our life – and we miss the opportunity to repent or attempt to fix our ways.

Allah ﷻ explains this scenario very vividly in the following verses:

وَلَقَدْ أَرْسَلْنَا إِلَىٰٓ أُمَمٍ مِّن قَبْلِكَ فَأَخَذْنَـٰهُم بِٱلْبَأْسَآءِ وَٱلضَّرَّآءِ لَعَلَّهُمْ يَتَضَرَّعُونَ ۝ فَلَوْلَآ إِذْ جَآءَهُم بَأْسُنَا تَضَرَّعُوا۟ وَلَـٰكِن قَسَتْ قُلُوبُهُمْ وَزَيَّنَ لَهُمُ ٱلشَّيْطَـٰنُ مَا كَانُوا۟ يَعْمَلُونَ ۝ فَلَمَّا نَسُوا۟ مَا ذُكِّرُوا۟ بِهِۦ فَتَحْنَا عَلَيْهِمْ أَبْوَٰبَ كُلِّ شَىْءٍ حَتَّىٰٓ إِذَا فَرِحُوا۟ بِمَآ أُوتُوٓا۟ أَخَذْنَـٰهُم بَغْتَةً فَإِذَا هُم مُّبْلِسُونَ ۝

*Wa-laqad arsalna ila umamim min qablika fa-akhadhnahum
bi'l-ba'sa'i wa'l-darra'i la'allahum yatadarra'un. Fa-lawla
idh ja'ahum ba'suna tadarra'u wa-lakin qasat qulubuhum
wazayyana lahum'l-shaytanu ma kanu ya'malun. Fa-lamma
nasu ma dhukiru bihi fatahna 'alayhim abwaba kulli shay'in
hatta idha farihu bima utu akhadhnahum baghtatan fa-idha
hum mublisun.*

"Indeed, We have sent messengers before you (O Prophet)
to other people who We put through suffering and adver-
sity for their denial, so perhaps they would be humbled.
Why did they not humble themselves when We made
them suffer? Instead, their hearts were hardened, and
Shaytan made their misdeeds appealing to them. When
they became oblivious to warnings, We showered them
with everything they desired. But just as they became
prideful of what they were given, We seized them by
surprise, then they instantly fell into despair!"
(*al-An'ām*, 6: 42-44)

Allah ﷻ sent punishments to people, but if they didn't change their
ways and turn to Allah ﷻ in repentance, Allah ﷻ removed their
hardships and gave them everything they wanted. This could also
be us. We could be disobeying Allah ﷻ day and night by backbiting, lying, cheating or by any other sinful means, yet when we ask
Allah ﷻ for something, He gives it to us. This is something that we
must be wary of. If we know that we are disobeying Allah ﷻ and we

are still getting everything we want, we must be aware that everything can be taken away from us in the blink of an eye and we may never get a chance to repent and change.

Sufyan al-Thawri said: "I disobey Allah ﷻ, and I see the result of it in the manners of my wife, my ride and even my servant."

Everything in our life is connected to Allah ﷻ because everything comes from Him and everything goes back to Him ﷻ.

Ahmad ibn Abi al-Hawari said that he told Abu Sulayman: "I missed Witr last night, and I did not pray the two sunnah of Fajr, and I did not pray Fajr in congregation." Abu Sulayman replied: "This is as a result of what you have done, as Allah ﷻ is not unjust to His servants, rather it is a desire that you fulfilled!"

Protection

One of the most important supplications we can make regarding this topic is:

اللَّهُمَّ إِنِّي أَسْأَلُكَ الْعَفْوَ وَالْعَافِيَةَ فِي دِينِي وَدُنْيَايَ وَأَهْلِي وَمَالِي

"O Allah ﷻ, I seek Your forgiveness and health (protection) in my religion, in my worldly affairs, in my family and in my wealth." (*Sahih Ibn Majah* 2/332)

We must keep asking Allah ﷻ to forgive us and to guide us away from sins and towards deeds that please Him, otherwise it can unfortunately become very easy to be led astray and have our sins affect us negatively in many ways.

Allah ﷻ tells us what the Prophet Nuh said to his people in the following ayāt:

فَقُلْتُ اسْتَغْفِرُوا رَبَّكُمْ إِنَّهُ كَانَ غَفَّارًا ۝ يُرْسِلِ السَّمَاءَ عَلَيْكُم مِّدْرَارًا ۝
وَيُمْدِدْكُم بِأَمْوَالٍ وَبَنِينَ وَيَجْعَل لَّكُمْ جَنَّاتٍ وَيَجْعَل لَّكُمْ أَنْهَارًا ۝

Fa-qultu istaghfiru rabbakum innahu kana ghaffaran. Yursi-li'l-sama'a 'alaykum midraran. Wa-yumdidkum bi-amwalin wa-banina wa-yaj'al lakum jannatin wa-yaj'al lakum anharan.

"And I (Nuh) said to them: 'Ask forgiveness of your Lord, indeed He is truly Most Forgiving. He will shower you with abundant rain. And increase you with wealth and children, and provide for you gardens and provide for you rivers.'" (*Surah Nuh*, 71:10-12)

We must ask Allah ﷻ for forgiveness so that we don't fall into repeated sins, and we don't become from amongst the losers in the Hereafter. Our connection with Allah ﷻ is based upon us putting in the effort; we must establish it and water it regularly for us to be able to keep this connection. If we do not do this, then we can be replaced by people who are a lot better than us – they will seek Allah's ﷻ forgiveness and guidance whilst we were too arrogant and stuck in our sinful ways.

When we ask Allah ﷻ for forgiveness after committing a sin, we should make the intention never to repeat it again and follow it up with a good deed, then *insha'aAllah* it will be as though we never committed the sin. However, if we do not do this and carry on sinning, then the reality is that we should expect to see the unpleasant results of our sinful deeds during our lifetime.

Chapter 4

Sins Weaken our Relationship with Allah

The heart is the centre of all good and bad.

A-faman sharaha Allahu sadrahu l'l-Islami fa-huwa 'ala nurin min rabbih. Fa-waylun li'l-qasiyati qulubuhum min dhikr Allahi. Ula'ika fi dalalin mubin.

"Can the misguided be like those whose hearts Allah has opened to Islam, so they are enlightened by their Lord? So, woe to those whose hearts are hardened at the remembrance of Allah! It is they who are clearly astray." (*al-Zumar*, 39:22)

When we stay away from sins our hearts stay alive and it is the best thing that we can do for our *akhirah* because we are going against what our *nafs* wants. It is a lot easier to give in to our *nafs* and commit sins, but fighting the urge and not giving in to our *nafs* is highly commendable and will be rewarded greatly by Allah.

We all have a relationship with Allah, but not all of us will have a good relationship with Him. Every time we sin, our relationship with Allah ﷻ becomes weaker – just as our relationship would change and become weaker with a good friend who repeatedly disappoints us. The more we are involved in sin, the more the means to become closer to Allah ﷻ are removed. However, it is not Allah ﷻ Who is giving up on us; He does not push us away. Rather, it is our sins that cause us to distance ourselves from Him.

The following Hadith *qudsi* provides a wonderful insight into strengthening our relationship with Allah ﷻ through obedience:

Abu Hurayrah, may Allah be pleased with him, reported that the Messenger of Allah ﷺ said: "Allah ﷻ the Exalted has said: 'I will declare war against him who treats with hostility a pious worshipper of Mine. And the most beloved thing with which My slave comes nearer to Me is what I have enjoined upon him, and My slave keeps on coming closer to Me through performing *nawafil* (voluntary prayers or extra deeds besides what is obligatory) until I love him, (so much so that) I become his hearing with which he hears, and his sight with which he sees, and his hand with which he strikes, and his leg with which he walks. And if he asks Me something, I will surely give it to him, and if he seeks My Protection (refuge), I will surely protect him.'" (*al-Bukhari*, and Hadith no. 38 in *Forty Hadith of al-Nawawi*)

We learn from this Hadith that fulfilling our obligations, such as *salah*, fasting, *zakat* and *hijab,* are starting points that put us on the path to becoming closer to Allah ﷻ. We can continuously become closer to Allah ﷻ by doing extra deeds. This doesn't imply that we only do extra deeds during Ramadan or on certain days, but continuously throughout the year. It is a process that we go through to reach the stage where Allah ﷻ loves us. Allah ﷻ also mentions that He becomes our hearing, our eyesight, our hands, and our legs once we have reached the point of Him loving us. But what does this mean? We won't be able to listen to anything that Allah ﷻ does not like, we won't be able to look at things that Allah ﷻ does not like, we won't be able to do actions with our hands which Allah 🌟 does not like and our legs will not take us anywhere that Allah 🌟 does not like. When our relationship with Allah 🌟 reaches this level, we find that we hate sins and distance ourselves as far as possible from them.

However, it is equally as important for us to understand that we will not have a strong connection with Allah 🌟 if we are continuously disobeying Him. This disconnect will be entirely our own doing; our sins sever our connection with Allah 🌟, Who always provides us with the chance to repent and strengthen our relationship with Him.

As our sins build up, they will gradually weaken our relationship with Allah 🌟, and every sin will produce another sin. Amr ibn al-ʿAs narrated a beautiful Hadith in which the Messenger of Allah said 🌟: "Verily, *iman* inside your hearts will wear off the same way clothes wear off! So, ask Allah 🌟 to renew the *iman* inside your hearts." (*al-Hakim*)

Sins weaken our *iman* and thus weaken our relationship with Allah 🌟. How often do we make *duʿa* for our relationship with Allah 🌟? The Prophet Muhammad 🌟 provided us with a wonderful *duʿa* that we should include regularly in our *adhkar*. Anas ibn Malik reported that Allah's Messenger 🌟 often said: "O You who turns the hearts about, establish my heart in Your religion." Anas said: "Prophet of God 🌟, do you fear for us who believe in you and in your message?" He replied: "Yes. The hearts are between two of God's fingers and He turns them about as He 🌟 wills." (*al-Tirmidhi and Ibn Majah*)

We could wake up one morning, pray Fajr on time, recite the Qur'an, do our morning remembrance and generally be doing good things, but when we leave the house, we may become involved in actions that are displeasing to Allah 🌟. Therefore, this *duʿa* is one of the most common supplications of the Prophet 🌟 because our hearts can so easily be changed. This *duʿa* is one we should make every day, even after we have sinned, because it is only due to a change in our hearts that we have committed the sin in the first instance.

Shaytan and his army will always work to damage our relationship with Allah ﷻ; they come and analyse our weaknesses and use those weaknesses to take us further away from Allah ﷻ. Every time we sin, we are obeying Shaytan and disobeying Allah ﷻ.

The stronger the relationship we have with Allah ﷻ, the happier and more obedient we will be. We will become content, even if we have very little in material wealth. Likewise, the weaker our relationship with Allah ﷻ, the more miserable our life will be, no matter how much we own or earn.

Allah ﷻ says in the Qur'an:

In yad'una min dunihi illa inathan wa-in yad'una illa shaytanan maridan. La'anahu'-Llahu wa-qala la-attakhidhanna min 'ibadika nasiban mafrudan.

"They call upon instead of Him none but female deities and they call upon none but a rebellious Shaytan. Whom Allah has cursed, for he had said: 'I will surely take from among Your servants a specific portion.'"
(*al-Nisa'*, 4: 117-118)

After Allah ﷻ cursed Shaytan, Shaytan said that he would take a share from each of us – meaning that he would find a weakness in us and use it to cause us to disobey Allah ﷻ. When we take some time to think about this properly, we will understand that Shaytan does indeed have some influence on us.

Whenever we obey Shaytan, our relationship with him becomes stronger, and we become more distant from Allah ﷻ. We are quick to blame others for our mistakes, but we should blame nobody but ourselves for committing sins. People can complain about the way we look, or the way we dress, or the deeds and actions that we do, they can push as much as they want to disobey Allah 🕮, but ultimately, it is down to us whether we choose to obey or disobey Him 🕮.

Consider this relationship like a triangle, with Allah 🕮 at one point, humans at another and Shaytan at another. Every time we disobey Allah 🕮, the distance between us and Him gets longer, whilst the distance between us and Shaytan becomes shorter. However, when we obey Allah 🕮, the distance between us and Him becomes shorter and the distance between us and Shaytan becomes longer.

Allah 🕮 told His servants: "I have honoured your father (Adam, peace be upon him), and raised his status, and preferred him to others. I ordered My angels to prostrate to him, as a sign of honour to him, and they obeyed Me, except My enemy and his enemy (Iblis). So how could you take him and his offspring as your allies besides Me, and how dare you obey him and disobey Me while he is your archenemy? You have followed My enemy after I had commanded you to take him as your enemy. You know that whoever befriends the enemy of the King is also considered the enemy of the King, for love and obedience cannot be fulfilled except by manifesting enmity towards the enemies of the Obeyed (Allah 🕮) and by joining His supporters." (*Ibn Al-Qayyim*)

This is a profound statement attributed to Allah 🕮, and one that we should always keep in our hearts and minds. If we obey Shaytan, we are taking him as a friend and are creating enmity with Allah 🕮, our Creator. We need to decide who we are going to take as a companion every day of our lives, Shaytan or Allah 🕮? Shaytan will try to influence us when we are alone and when we are in the company of others.

Sins can affect our relationship with Allah 🕮 to such an extent that we reach a point where we give up trying and our sins become worse. We become weaker and are unable to put in the effort to better ourselves and our relationship with Allah ﷻ. We can compare this to hiking up a hill or mountain; making our way up is difficult as it requires endurance and effort, we need to build up momentum, but we also develop a willingness to do more and create a positive energy. However, going downhill is easy, and the moment we sin, we are slipping away quickly and furthering our distance from Allah ﷻ.

Ibn Abi'l-Dunya said: "Allah ﷻ revealed to Yusha' ibn Nun: 'I am destroying forty thousand of your best people, and sixty thousand of your evil people.' He replied: 'O Lord, those are evil people, but why should You destroy the good people?' Allah ﷻ said: 'Because they were never angry when I was angry with those that disobeyed Me, but instead they used to socialise (eat and drink) with them.'"

When we are socialising with someone who is obviously disobeying Allah ﷻ and we tell ourselves that they will change or that we are going to change them, what guarantee do we have that they will not end up changing us for the worse?

I would like to mention a story of a young man (from more modern times), who lived in Madinah. Whilst living in Madinah, he didn't come across any female without *hijab*. He then travelled to Egypt and at the airport he saw a female without *hijab*, and he fainted. When he regained consciousness, he was asked why he fainted, and he replied: "How can people disobey Allah ﷻ like this?"

This story should make us think about where we are in our relationship with Allah ﷻ. When we see Him being disobeyed, how does it affect us? Do we become angered or upset? The small, constant sins we commit harden our hearts and stop us from feeling anything when Allah ﷻ is disobeyed.

It all begins with the whispers of Shaytan, pulling at the strings of our *nafs*. We don't usually commit major sins overnight, as Shaytan works gradually to lead us away from Allah ﷻ. If a person stopped offering *salah*, it likely would have started from him not doing the Sunnah *rak'ah*, delaying *salah* or missing certain *salahs* during the day etc., finally reaching the point where he no longer prays anymore.

There is also another famous narration which fits in perfectly with this concept. There was a monk who lived alone in the mountains, and he had neighbours who were a brother and a sister, but he had never seen the sister as he was always in his home or room worshipping Allah ﷻ. One day, the brother needed to leave for a journey. He knocked on the door of the monk and asked him to check on his sister every now and then by knocking on the door. It was agreed that she wouldn't open the door but would let him know that she was okay. The monk knocked on the door every day, and after a few days, he heard her voice and was attracted to it. He then asked her to speak more. Slowly the requests began to increase, gradually developing into an illicit relationship, and eventually, she became pregnant. To conceal this sin, the monk killed and buried her. Upon the brother's return, the monk said to him that his sister ran away. However, the brother found out what happened and killed the monk.

Protection

Abd al-Wahhab ibn al-Ward narrated from a man among the inhabitants of Madinah, who said: "Mu'awiyah wrote a letter to A'ishah saying: 'Write a letter to advise me, and do not overburden me.' So A'ishah, may Allah ﷻ be pleased with her, wrote to Mu'awiyah: 'Peace be upon you. As for what follows, indeed, I heard the Messenger of Allah ﷺ saying: "Whoever seeks Allah's ﷻ pleasure by the people's wrath, Allah ﷻ will suffice him from the people. And whoever seeks the people's pleasure by Allah's ﷻ wrath, Allah will entrust him to the people. And peace be upon you".'" (*al-Tirmidhi*, 2414)

Mu'awiyah was the ruler of the people at the time he asked for advice from A'ishah, and the advice she gave was extremely befitting for someone in his position. She told him to never disobey Allah ﷻ in order to please people, otherwise Allah ﷻ would leave him to suffer at the hands of the people. However, even if people become displeased with him whilst he is obeying Allah ﷻ, Allah ﷻ will always protect him from them.

We sin because of three reasons: ourselves, Shaytan and people. When we worry too much about what people will say, or when we give in to the pressure of other people's comments and misguidance, we fall into sin.

If we want our relationship with Allah ﷻ to be strong, we should focus on pleasing Him only. When thinking about what will bring us closer to Allah ﷻ, we must aim to make every action of ours pleasing to Him; our thoughts, our feelings and our movements must be in accordance with His pleasure. We should remind ourselves constantly that Allah ﷻ is All-Hearing and All-Seeing.

Our own connection with Allah ﷻ will also begin to become strong when we start practicing some of His attributes. For example, Allah ﷻ is The Ever-Forgiving. One of the most difficult things for us to do is to forgive others when they have wronged us. Yet, the greatest of all creation, the Messenger of Allah ﷺ, was insulted and physically hurt by the people, yet he still forgave them because he had a strong connection with Allah ﷻ. Allah ﷻ is also The Generous, and so we should also practice generosity. Generosity, for us, is not limited to giving money, but is also in other actions, such as sharing or giving away something that we love for ourselves (this could be something as simple as offering our parking space to someone else and parking our own car further away). We can be generous by giving more than what someone has asked us or by giving something before they have even made a request.

The closer we become to Allah ﷻ, the more of His attributes we can practice. Allah ﷻ is the Most Merciful, and we too can become merciful. One of the biggest signs of this attribute are our tears; we become tearful upon hearing or reciting the Qur'an or when we are alone and talking to Allah ﷻ. If we have dry eyes and do not cry in private (many people are unable to cry in public), then we must question where we have gone wrong as this is a sign of a hardened heart and one which is not benefiting of *rahmah* (mercy).

When the son of the beloved Prophet Muhammad ﷺ passed away, he cried and Sa'd ibn 'Ubadah asked him: "Even you, O Messenger of Allah ﷺ?" And the Prophet Muhammad ﷺ replied: "O Ibn 'Awf, this a mercy that Allah ﷻ made in the hearts of his servants. And verily, Allah ﷻ shows mercy to those of His servants who are merciful." (*al-Bukhari*)

A very famous and important Hadith regarding Allah's ﷻ mercy is narrated by Abu Sa'id al-Khudri. The Prophet ﷺ said: "Amongst the men of Banu Isra'il, there was a man who had murdered ninety-nine people. Then he set out asking (whether his repentance could be accepted or not). He came upon a monk and asked him if his repentance could be accepted, the monk replied in the negative and so the man killed him. He kept on asking until a man advised him to go to such and such a village. (So, he left for it), but death overtook him on the way. While dying, he turned his chest towards the village (where we had hoped his repentance would be accepted), and so the angels of mercy and the angels of punishment quarrelled amongst themselves regarding him. Allah ﷻ ordered the village (towards which he was going), to come closer to him and ordered the village (from where he came) to go far away, and then He ordered the angels to measure the distances between his body and the two villages. So, he was found to be one span closer to the village he was going to. So, he was forgiven." (*al-Bukhari*, 3470)

This man committed major sins by killing people, but he made the intention to change and repent, and so he was forgiven. He was advised to move away from where he lived, and this is something that we should also take into account for ourselves. The people we surround ourselves with have an influence on us, and if we find that we easily fall into sin, then we must move away from them. We can see very clearly through this Hadith that Allah ﷻ is All-Forgiving, and He loves to forgive. We are the ones who give up and do not put in the effort to improve our relationship with Allah ﷻ.

However, despite this, we mustn't abuse the fact that Allah ﷻ is All-Forgiving, failing to remember that He ﷻ can also punish severely:

وَيَسْتَعْجِلُونَكَ بِٱلسَّيِّئَةِ قَبْلَ ٱلْحَسَنَةِ وَقَدْ خَلَتْ مِن قَبْلِهِمُ ٱلْمَثُلَـٰتُ وَإِنَّ رَبَّكَ لَذُو مَغْفِرَةٍ لِّلنَّاسِ عَلَىٰ ظُلْمِهِمْ وَإِنَّ رَبَّكَ لَشَدِيدُ ٱلْعِقَابِ ۝

Wa-yasta'jilunaka bi'l-sayyi'ati qabla'l-hasanati wa-qad khalat min qablihimu'l-mathulatu wa-inna rabbaka ladhu maghfiratin l'l-nasi 'ala zulmihim wa-inna rabbaka lashadi-du'l-'iqab.

"They impatiently urge you to bring about evil before good, while there has already occurred before them similar punishments (to what they demand). And indeed, your Lord is the Possessor of forgiveness for the people despite their wrongdoing, and indeed, your Lord is severe in penalty." (*al-Ra'd*, 13: 6)

So, how do we know that our relationship with Allah ﷻ is good?

1. Obeying Allah ﷻ becomes easy, and we don't struggle to do good deeds.
2. Allah ﷻ brings to us the opportunities to obey Him and we take advantage of them and do good.
3. We don't like or enjoy disobedience to Allah ﷻ, and our hearts even dislike the thought of disobeying Allah ﷻ.

Contrastingly, how do we know that our relationship with Allah is not good?

1. Once we disobey Him, many more doors of disobedience open up and it becomes easy to fall into sin. It could be something as simple as turning on the TV to watch the news, but we end up watching something haram.
2. We become lazy or arrogant and don't want to change ourselves for the better.
3. Our hearts become hardened, and this carries on until we have a dead heart. We no longer feel anything when committing a sin.

When a person has living heart, a heart connected to Allah, and they commit even a small sin or think about committing a sin, it will feel as though they have lost something valuable - as though they are losing their relationship with Allah.

May Allah soften our hearts and make us of those who please Him. Amin.

Chapter 5

Sins Strengthen Our Relationship with Shaytan

Allah ﷻ says: "And he to whom Shaytan is a companion - then evil is he as a companion!" (*al-Nisa'*, 4:38)

In the previous chapter, we learnt that sins weaken our relationship with Allah ﷻ and strengthen our relationship with Shaytan. But, who is Shaytan? Allah ﷻ refers to him as both Shaytan and Iblis in the Qur'an; he is referred to as Iblis eleven times and as Shaytan (singular) or *shayatin* (plural) eighty-eight times.

Like all of the names given to things in the *din*, such words have a linguistic root meaning which serve the purpose of giving further insight into their definitions. For example, when we look at what *salah* is and the meaning of it, it is derived from صلة (*silah*), which means connection. And so, *salah* is actually our connection with Allah ﷻ. The root of the name Iblis is بلس (ba-la-sa), and there are three meanings we can derive from it:

1.   The first broad meaning is to "remain in grief". This is because Iblis will never set foot in Jannah again. There is no doubt that Iblis, along with his army of *shayatin*, will have Jahannam as their eternal abode after the Day of Judgement. Allah ﷻ told Iblis that he was expelled from Jannah in the following verse:

Qala fa'khruj minha fa-innaka rajim.

"Allah ﷻ said: 'Then depart from it (Jannah), for indeed, you are expelled.'"   (*al-Hijr*, 15: 34)

Iblis was a part of Jannah and held an honourable role, but he was thrown out, never to return. This should also serve as a reminder to us that we cannot say to anyone, no matter how much they may have sinned, that they will not enter Jannah. Such people are not referred to as Iblis by Allah ﷻ or the Prophet Muhammad ﷺ, rather they are referred to as disbelievers, sinners or disobedient.

2.   The second meaning is "he despaired." This means that he has lost the mercy of Allah ﷻ, and it is impossible for him to benefit from that mercy. It is possible, however, for everyone else to benefit from the mercy of Allah ﷻ.

3.   The third meaning is تلبيس (*talbis*), which is translated as "confusion". Two lessons can be taken from this meaning: (a) that Iblis himself is confused and (b) that his job is to confuse us. When we become confused by questioning what is right or wrong, or whether something is from the Qur'an and Sunnah, or why we should do something, this is all from Iblis.

Apart from Shaytan and Iblis, he is also known as Abu Murrah, which means Father of Bitterness. He was given this name as he became bitter after the creation of Adam and after being expelled from Jannah forever, whilst *we* have the opportunity to attain Jannah even after sinning. Another name is *Aduww Allah*, which means Enemy of Allah ﷻ. He will remain the enemy of Allah ﷻ forever, and so he will remain our enemy forever.

When looking into which category of creation Shaytan belongs to, the most correct opinion is that he was from the jinn. This is due to Allah ﷻ mentioning this in the following verse:

وَإِذْ قُلْنَا لِلْمَلَـٰٓئِكَةِ ٱسْجُدُوا۟ لِءَادَمَ فَسَجَدُوٓا۟ إِلَّآ إِبْلِيسَ كَانَ مِنَ ٱلْجِنِّ
فَفَسَقَ عَنْ أَمْرِ رَبِّهِ ۗ ... ﴿٥٠﴾

Wa-idh qulna li'l-mala'ikati usjudu li-adama fa-sajadu illa
iblisa kana mina'l-jinni fa-fasaqa 'an amri rabbihi

"And [mention] when We said to the angels: 'Prostrate to
Adam,' and they prostrated, except for Iblis. He was of the
jinn and departed from [i.e., disobeyed] the command of
his Lord." (*al-Kahf*, 18: 50)

Angels never disobey Allah ﷻ, nor have they been given any choice
in the matter of obedience, whereas humans and jinn have been
given the will to obey or disobey.

Another important aspect of Shaytan that we must take into
account is how close he is to us at all times. Anas ibn Malik, may
Allah ﷻ be pleased with him, reported that the Messenger of Allah
said: "The devil flows in a man like his blood." (*Bukhari and Muslim*)

If we look at the above Hadith, we can understand that it is indeed
a profound statement, but what is the meaning behind it? Delving
deeper, we realise that the answer to this question lies in fasting.
When we fast, we become dehydrated and so our blood vessels become narrower. This in turn will make it more difficult for Shaytan
to move and influence us. When we fast, we keep away from things
that Allah ﷻ has prohibited, otherwise our fasting becomes invalid.

Ensuring that we stay away from Shaytan is a huge task for us all.
But Allah ﷻ gives us hope and tells us which people are able to stay
away from Shaytan and, therefore, closer to Him:

إِنَّ ٱلَّذِينَ ٱتَّقَوا۟ إِذَا مَسَّهُمْ طَـٰٓئِفٌ مِّنَ ٱلشَّيْطَـٰنِ تَذَكَّرُوا۟ فَإِذَا هُم مُّبْصِرُونَ ﴿٢٠١﴾

Inna'l-ladhina ittaqaw idha massahum ta'-ifun mina'l- shay-
tani tadhakkaru fa-idha hum mubsirun.

"Indeed, those who fear Allah ﷻ – when an impulse touches them from Shaytan, they remember [Him] and at once they have insight." (*al-A'raf*, 7: 201)

The more we become close to Allah ﷻ, the further away Shaytan is from us. When we are sinning, we are distancing ourselves from Allah ﷻ in that moment, and Shaytan attacks us like easy prey.

The whispering of Shaytan is also mentioned in the last chapter of the Qur'an:

Min sharri'l-waswasi'l-khannas.

"From the evil of the lurking [retreating] whisperer." (*al-Nas*, 114: 4)

Al-waswas means that he whispers. For example, he puts thoughts into our mind, encouraging us to choose wrong over right actions. However, when we seek refuge in Allah ﷻ from Shaytan, he will become *al-khannas*, which means that he will retreat and become weaker in his attacks on us. However, he will not disappear completely from our lives until we die.

One sin that is directly related to Shaytan is the showing of arrogance. Shaytan showed arrogance when Allah ﷻ commanded him to prostrate before the Prophet Adam, may Allah ﷻ be pleased with him:

$$\text{وَإِذْ قُلْنَا لِلْمَلَـٰٓئِكَةِ ٱسْجُدُوا۟ لِءَادَمَ فَسَجَدُوٓا۟ إِلَّآ إِبْلِيسَ أَبَىٰ وَٱسْتَكْبَرَ وَكَانَ مِنَ ٱلْكَـٰفِرِينَ}$$

Wa-idh qulna li'l-mala'ikat usjudu li-adama fa-sajadu illa iblisa aba wa'stakbara wa-kana min'l-kafirin.

"And [mention] when We said to the angels: 'Prostrate before Adam,' so they prostrated, except for Iblis. He refused

and was arrogant and became of the disbelievers."
(*al-Baqarah*, 2: 34)

Arrogance is a part of Iblis's character, and so every single time that
we show arrogance, we are in fact following his footsteps and taking him as our example. Arrogance does not always show through
our words, but it can also manifest itself through our feelings and
thoughts. For example, we may feel happy if we see or come across
someone in the *masjid* who is from the same or similar ethnicity to
ourselves, but we don't feel the same happiness if someone from a
different ethnicity comes to sit next to us. In fact, we start wishing
that they would go and sit somewhere else – this shows we have
arrogance in our heart. The concept of bullying is also based on arrogance because a bully will believe they are better than their victim,
just as Iblis thought he was better than the Prophet Adam when he
refused to prostrate to him.

Furthermore, Allah ﷻ tells us in the Qur'an that Shaytan is our
enemy, so taking him as our enemy should be our only option.

إِنَّ ٱلشَّيْطَـٰنَ لَكُمْ عَدُوٌّ فَٱتَّخِذُوهُ عَدُوًّا إِنَّمَا يَدْعُوا۟ حِزْبَهُۥ
لِيَكُونُوا۟ مِنْ أَصْحَـٰبِ ٱلسَّعِيرِ ۝

Inna'l-shaytana lakum 'aduwwun fa'ttakhidhuhu 'aduwwan
innama yad'u hizbahu li-yakunu min ashabi'l-sa'ir.

"Surely Shaytan is an enemy to you, so take him as an enemy. He only invites his followers to become inmates of the
Blaze." (*Fatir,* 35: 6)

Our relationship with Shaytan should be limited to this enmity. He
is our enemy because he is constantly working to make us disobey
our Creator. Shaytan always remains our enemy: before, during and
after Ramadan, wherever we are in the world and whether we are in
Makkah or sitting in a *masjid*.

The Tricks of Shaytan

Shaytan gets us to disobey Allah ﷻ by going against His commands and committing evil or immoral actions. He also gets us to think about Allah ﷻ or say things about Allah ﷻ that are not befitting. For example, whenever we think that something isn't fair, we are in fact thinking negatively of Allah ﷻ.

Whenever we find ourselves complaining about certain aspects of our body or face, we are in fact complaining about the way that Allah ﷻ has created us. And this is exactly what Shaytan wants us to do. He wants us to be unhappy with our nose or our teeth and to such an extent that we not only consider but take action to alter the way Allah ﷻ originally created us.

The Prophet ﷺ taught us a wonderful supplication that we should make when we look at ourselves in the mirror: "Ya Allah ﷻ, just as You have beautified me externally, beautify me internally." This does not exhibit arrogance, but rather is a declaration that Allah ﷻ has created us in the best way and so we are in need of asking Him to beautify our inside too. We should all have a good level of self-esteem, otherwise Shaytan will take every opportunity to lower our self-esteem and make us want to change the way we look. We shouldn't wait for others to comment on us and tell us that we are beautiful, we should lift ourselves up first and foremost.

Other sins that Shaytan gets people to commit include drinking alcohol, taking or smoking drugs, gambling, going to so-called fortune tellers etc. Allah ﷻ tells us that these sins are from Shaytan, and by doing these sins, Shaytan creates hatred between us and other people. Every time that we obey Shaytan, we are taking him as a friend, and ruining our relationship with Allah ﷻ and others.

The influence of Shaytan does not stop here. He can also play a part in the company that we keep. Allah ﷻ tells us this in the following ayah:

وَإِذَا رَأَيْتَ ٱلَّذِينَ يَخُوضُونَ فِىٓ ءَايَٰتِنَا فَأَعْرِضْ عَنْهُمْ حَتَّىٰ يَخُوضُواْ فِى
حَدِيثٍ غَيْرِهِۦ ۚ وَإِمَّا يُنسِيَنَّكَ ٱلشَّيْطَٰنُ فَلَا تَقْعُدْ بَعْدَ ٱلذِّكْرَىٰ مَعَ
ٱلْقَوْمِ ٱلظَّٰلِمِينَ ۝

Wa-idha ra'ayta'l-ladhina yakhuduna fi ayatina fa'a'rid 'anhum
hatta yakhudu fi hadithin ghayri. Wa-imma yunsiyannaka'l-shay-
tanu fa-la taq'ud ba'ada'l-dhikra ma'a'l-qawmi'l-zalimin.

"And when you come across those who ridicule Our
revelations, turn away from them until they engage in a
different topic. Should Shaytan make you forget, then once
you remember, do not continue to sit with the wrongdoing
people." (*al-An'am*, 6: 68)

Allah ﷻ clearly mentions here that if we see people discussing the
din in a negative or offensive manner, we should not sit with them
as they are bad company. If Shaytan makes us forget this at first, but
we later remember, then we should leave immediately. When we
find ourselves in bad company, we should ask why we are in such a
situation. We make it easy for Shaytan to have an influence on us,
and thus we end up amongst people who are also greatly affected by
Shaytan. However, as soon as we realise this, we should work hard
to push Shaytan far away from ourselves. And the best way to remove him is by reconnecting with Allah ﷻ – there is no other way,
as we are either with Allah ﷻ or we are with Shaytan and our *nafs*.

Not only does Shaytan push us towards bad company, but he also
pushes us to argue with one another. Allah ﷻ says in the Qur'an:

وَإِنَّ ٱلشَّيَٰطِينَ لَيُوحُونَ إِلَىٰٓ أَوْلِيَآئِهِمْ لِيُجَٰدِلُوكُمْ ۖ وَإِنْ
أَطَعْتُمُوهُمْ إِنَّكُمْ لَمُشْرِكُونَ ۝

Wa- inna'l-shayatina la-yuhuna ila awliya'ihim li-yujadilu-
kum wa-in ata'tumuhum innakum lamushrikun.

"And certainly, the devils whisper to their human associates
to argue with you. If you were to obey them, then you too,
would be polytheists." (*Surah al-An'am*, 6: 121)

Arguments happen all around us, all the time – whether it be between the young or old, siblings, parents and children, or people in
masjids or schools. This is one of the most used and powerful tools
of Shaytan and the reason why the Prophet Muhammad ﷺ said
(as narrated by Abu Umamah): "I guarantee a house in the surroundings of Paradise for a person who avoids quarrelling, even if
he were in the right." (*Abu Dawud*, 4800)

Whenever we find ourselves in a situation in which we are arguing
and we start to feel uncomfortable or we have the urge to carry on
and say something offensive, we need to do our best to resist this
urge to defeat Shaytan and his army. Avoiding arguments does not
make us weak, on the contrary, it shows that we have the strength
to withhold ourselves even if we are right. We don't want to allow
Shaytan the chance to have an influence on us.

Arguments can also lead to misguidance, which has been Shaytan's main aim since the creation of Adam and will remain so until
the last day. When someone asks us why we are not doing certain
actions according to Islam, we usually start arguing, becoming angry
and making excuses. It seldom happens that someone will admit that
they are weak or ask to be taught about what is pleasing to Allah ﷻ.

We are told in the Qur'an:

*Fariqan hada wa-fariqan haqqa 'alayhim'l-dalalatu innahum
ittakhadhu'l-shayatina awliya'a min duni'l-lahi wa-yahsabuna annahum muhtadun.*

"A group of you He guided, and a group destined to stray. They have taken devils as their allies instead of Allah – thinking they are rightly guided." (*al-A'raf*, 7: 30)

We should ask Allah ﷻ to make us sincere in our actions and intentions so that we only do that which pleases Him. Umar ibn al-Khattab, may Allah ﷻ be pleased with him, said: "We know only the external, the internal is with Allah ﷻ." Sincerity is one of the best things we can be given by Allah ﷻ as it means we are motivated by the pleasure of Allah ﷻ, rather than the opinion of people. When we start worrying about what others think of us, it is Shaytan putting those thoughts in our head. And by letting those worries get to us, he uses this further to his advantage and makes us insincere in our intentions and actions.

Another trick of Shaytan is to encourage us to abandon the Qur'an. By pushing us away from the Qur'an, Shaytan stops us from understanding the lessons that Allah ﷻ has provided throughout it. However, if each one of us took the time to only learn and understand *Surah al-Ikhlas* completely, Shaytan would be greatly weakened.

We are given a wonderful parable in the Qur'an in the following verses:

وَٱتْلُ عَلَيْهِمْ نَبَأَ ٱلَّذِىٓ ءَاتَيْنَٰهُ ءَايَٰتِنَا فَٱنسَلَخَ مِنْهَا فَأَتْبَعَهُ ٱلشَّيْطَٰنُ فَكَانَ مِنَ ٱلْغَاوِينَ ۩ وَلَوْ شِئْنَا لَرَفَعْنَٰهُ بِهَا وَلَٰكِنَّهُۥٓ أَخْلَدَ إِلَى ٱلْأَرْضِ وَٱتَّبَعَ هَوَىٰهُ فَمَثَلُهُۥ كَمَثَلِ ٱلْكَلْبِ إِن تَحْمِلْ عَلَيْهِ يَلْهَثْ أَوْ تَتْرُكْهُ يَلْهَث ذَّٰلِكَ مَثَلُ ٱلْقَوْمِ ٱلَّذِينَ كَذَّبُوا۟ بِـَٔايَٰتِنَا فَٱقْصُصِ ٱلْقَصَصَ لَعَلَّهُمْ يَتَفَكَّرُونَ ۩

Watlu 'alayhim naba'a'l-ladhi ataynahu ayatina fa'nsalakha minha fa-atba'ahu'l- shaytanu fa-kana mina'l-ghawin. Wa law shi'na larafa'nahu biha wa-lkinnahu akhlada ila'l-ar-di wa'ttaba'a hawahu. Fa-mathaluhu ka-mathali'l-kalbi in

*tahmil 'alayhi yalhath aw tatrukhu yalhath. Dhalika math-
alu'l-qawmi'l-ladhina kadhabu bi-ayatina fa'qsusi'l-qasasa
la'allahum yatafakarun.*

"And relate to them [O Muhammad] the story of the one
to whom We gave Our signs, but he abandoned them, so
Shaytan took hold of him and became a deviant. If We had
willed, We would have elevated him with Our signs, but he
clung to this life – following his evil desires. His example
is that of a dog; if you chase it away it pants, and if you
leave it, it still pants. This is the example of the people who
deny Our signs. So, narrate to them stories of the past, so
perhaps they will reflect." (*al-A'raf*, 7: 175-176)

When Allah ﷻ describes the person as moving away from His signs,
this means to move away from the Qur'an. Moving away from the
Qur'an can happen due to several excuses that Shaytan puts into
our minds, such as it is too difficult to read, or we don't have enough
time. When we put the Qur'an on the shelf and only bring it down
to read on certain occasions, Shaytan will stay attached to us. But
when we put our own desires and our preference for this worldly
life aside, reciting the Qur'an and living according to its teachings,
Allah ﷻ will elevate us to a lofty status.

Allah ﷻ uses the parable of a dog in these verses because a dog will
always be panting, whether he is stationary or being chased away.
When comparing this to ourselves, it means that we have been giv-
en the Qur'an, but we don't use it, and by not using it, it is as if we
don't have it as a sign. In both cases, we are misguided.

Jealousy is another act and emotion that Shaytan puts into the
hearts of people to strengthen their relationship with him. A great
example of this is given in *Surah Yusuf*:

قَالَ يَٰبُنَىَّ لَا تَقْصُصْ رُءْيَاكَ عَلَىٰٓ إِخْوَتِكَ فَيَكِيدُوا۟ لَكَ كَيْدًا إِنَّ
ٱلشَّيْطَٰنَ لِلْإِنسَٰنِ عَدُوٌّ مُّبِينٌ ۝

*Qala ya bunayya la taqsus ru'yaka 'ala ikhwatika fayakidu
laka kaydan inna'l-shaytana li'l-insani 'aduwwun mubin.*

"He replied: 'O my dear son! Do not relate your vision to
your brothers, or they will devise a plot against you. Surely
Shaytan is a sworn enemy to humankind.'" (*Yusuf*, 12:5)

The Prophet Ya'qub, may Allah ﷻ be pleased with him, knew that
telling others of such a big dream – even close family – could prove
detrimental for his son, Prophet Yusuf. He knew that Shaytan
would use any given opportunity to misguide people, and if he was
to mention his dream to his brothers, Shaytan would have made
them jealous and thus plot against him. From this, we learn that we
should always be wary of sharing too much or sharing anything that
could cause jealousy in others. Instead, it is often better to withhold
speech, make du'a for others and protect them from being affected
by Shaytan.

Ironically, we do not like being betrayed by others as it causes dis-
appointment, anger and pain, yet we are willingly being betrayed by
Shaytan. On the Day of Judgement, we will be made to face such
betrayal as told in the following verse:

وَقَالَ ٱلشَّيْطَٰنُ لَمَّا قُضِىَ ٱلْأَمْرُ إِنَّ ٱللَّهَ وَعَدَكُمْ وَعْدَ ٱلْحَقِّ وَوَعَدتُّكُمْ
فَأَخْلَفْتُكُمْ ۖ وَمَا كَانَ لِىَ عَلَيْكُم مِّن سُلْطَٰنٍ إِلَّآ أَن دَعَوْتُكُمْ فَٱسْتَجَبْتُمْ
لِى ۖ فَلَا تَلُومُونِى وَلُومُوٓا۟ أَنفُسَكُم ۖ مَّآ أَنَا۠ بِمُصْرِخِكُمْ وَمَآ أَنتُم بِمُصْرِخِىَّ ۖ إِنِّى
كَفَرْتُ بِمَآ أَشْرَكْتُمُونِ مِن قَبْلُ ۗ إِنَّ ٱلظَّٰلِمِينَ لَهُمْ عَذَابٌ أَلِيمٌ ۝

*Wa-qala'l-shaytanu lamma qudiya'l-amru inna'l-laha
wa'adakum wa'da'l-haqqi wa-wa'adtukum fa-akhlaftukum
wa-ma kana liya 'alaykum min sultanin illa an da'awtukum
fa'stajabtum li fa-la talumuni wa-lumu anfusakum ma ana
bi-musrikhikum wa-ma antum bi-musrikhiyy inni kafartu
bima ashraktumuni min qablu inna'l-dhalimina lahum
'adhabun alim.*

"And Shaytan will say to his followers after the judgement has been passed: 'Indeed, Allah ﷻ has made you a true promise. I too made you a promise, but I betrayed you. I did not have any authority over you. I only called you and you responded to me. So do not blame me, blame yourselves. I cannot save you, nor can you save me. Indeed, I denounce your previous association of me with Allah ﷻ.' Surely, the wrongdoers will suffer a painful punishment." (*Ibrahim*, 14: 22)

Another trick of Shaytan is to cause us to use bad words, which also affects the people we are talking to. We must speak in the best way possible by being polite and well-mannered, as Shaytan will always be nudging us and whispering to us to use impolite or foul language. If we hear others using bad language outside in public, rather than looking down upon them, we should make du'a for them so that Allah ﷻ removes the influence of Shaytan from them and protects our children from learning such language. Allah ﷻ tells us of the importance of speaking in the best manner in the Qur'an:

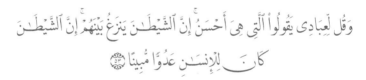

Waqul li-'ibadi yaqulu'l-lati hiya ahsan. Inna'l-shaytana yan-zaghu baynahum inna'l-shaytana kana li'l-insani 'aduwwan mubinan.

"And tell My believing servants to say only what is best. Shaytan certainly seeks to sow discord among them. Shaytan is indeed a sworn enemy to humankind."
(*al-Isra'*, 17: 53)

Shaytan does not only influence the way we interact with people, but he also influences the actions we do, which can, in turn, have a negative impact on those around us and our surrounding environment. By making us become wasteful, we are also becoming the brothers and sisters of Shaytan, as Allah ﷻ has mentioned in the following verses:

وَءَاتِ ذَا ٱلْقُرْبَىٰ حَقَّهُۥ وَٱلْمِسْكِينَ وَٱبْنَ ٱلسَّبِيلِ وَلَا تُبَذِّرْ تَبْذِيرًا ۝ إِنَّ ٱلْمُبَذِّرِينَ كَانُوٓاْ إِخْوَٰنَ ٱلشَّيَٰطِينِ ۖ وَكَانَ ٱلشَّيْطَٰنُ لِرَبِّهِۦ كَفُورًا ۝

Waati dha'l-qurba haqqahu wa'l-miskina wa'bna'l-sabili wa-la tubadhir tabdhiran. Inna'l-mubadhirina kanu ikhwana'l-shayatini wa-kana'l-shaytanu li-rabbihi kafuran.

"Give to close relatives their due, as well as the poor and needy travellers, and do not spend wastefully. Surely, the wasteful are like brothers to the devils. And Shaytan is ever ungrateful to his Lord." (*al-Isra'*, 17: 26-27)

It doesn't matter how rich we are, or how much of something we have, we should not be wasteful. Whether it is food, water, electricity, time, or other resources, Shaytan loves us to be wasteful and through this brings us so close to him that Allah ﷻ describes us as being his brothers and sisters.

Finally, I would like to end this chapter on a very important point. Neglecting the remembrance of Allah ﷻ can cause us to become blinded, allowing Shaytan to get a very strong hold of us and preventing us from receiving the light of the *din*.

Allah ﷻ says:

وَمَن يَعْشُ عَن ذِكْرِ ٱلرَّحْمَٰنِ نُقَيِّضْ لَهُۥ شَيْطَٰنًا فَهُوَ لَهُۥ قَرِينٌ ۝ وَإِنَّهُمْ لَيَصُدُّونَهُمْ عَنِ ٱلسَّبِيلِ وَيَحْسَبُونَ أَنَّهُم مُّهْتَدُونَ ۝

Wa-man ya'shu 'an dhikri'l-rahmani nuqayyid lahu shaytanan fahuwa lahu qarin. Wa-innahum layasuddunahum 'ani'l-sabili wa-yahsabuna annahum muhtadun.

> "And whoever turns a blind eye from the remembrance of the Most Merciful, We appoint for him a devil, and he is to him a close companion. And indeed, they [the devils] hinder them from the Right Way, while they think they are rightly guided."   (*al-Zukhruf,* 43: 36-37)

The word "*qarin*" in the above verse means close companion. If we do not remember Allah ﷻ enough, Shaytan becomes a close companion to us, like our shadow, and will be with us wherever we go to further misguide us. We will keep doing wrong, ignoring the commandments of Allah ﷻ and neglecting the remembrance of Him, whilst Shaytan will make us believe that we are on the Right Path.

May Allah ﷻ protect us and make us from those who learn and act upon what we learn and may Allah ﷻ make Shaytan so small for us that he has no influence on us. Amin.

Chapter 6
Sins cause Affliction

We seldom think about how our actions can affect our surrounding environment, but Allah ﷻ tells us that our deeds can be the cause of corruption on the earth in the following verse:

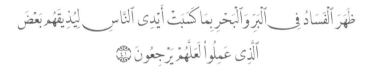

Zahara'l-fasadu fi'l-barri wa'l-bahri bi-ma kasabat aydi'l-na-si li-yudhiqahum ba'da'l-ladhi 'amilu la'allahum yarji'un.

"Corruption has spread on land and sea as a result of what people's hands have done, so that Allah may cause them to taste [the consequences of] some of their deeds and perhaps they might return [to the Right Path]."
(*al-Rum*, 30:41)

If we backbite about someone or say something negative about someone or something (especially without knowing the full truth), and then we witness a natural disaster a few days after, we don't associate it with what we have done. But disobeying Allah ﷻ can lead to calamities that affect everyone and the environment.

There are several factors that can count as corruption, and these are:

- *Shirk* - people disobey Allah ﷻ, associate things with Allah ﷻ and even leave the *din* completely. We and our children are exposed to this corruption in our surroundings on a regular basis.
- Killing people unjustly - there has been an increase in shootings, stabbings and other forms of killing in recent times to the extent that it happens almost daily.
- Hunger and famine - people do not distribute wealth and food fairly, causing many people to suffer.
- Lack of *barakah* - we see this in our time, our actions and even in the way we feel. For example, we may go to the supermarket today to do our full grocery shop, but the things we buy do not last long or they become spoiled quickly.
- An increase in the cost of living and a lack of resources - we see this in current times through things such as grocery prices, fuel prices, etc.
- Injustice - this isn't limited to injustice caused by the leadership of the countries that we live in, but it is also applicable to our homes. The way that we treat our children, and our spouses can also be susceptible to injustice. For example, we may want our spouse to do everything our way and be unwilling to compromise, not fulfilling their fair requests.
- Lack of rain (due to environmental disasters).
- Corruption in the sea can be found in the form of pollution (which affects the number and quality of fish available) and an increase of drowning or other accidents/disasters.

Commenting on this verse, Imam Ibn 'Ashur described corruption in the land as:

- Loss of what is beneficial and an abundance of harm. For example, we may struggle with unhappiness and we read or come across bad news daily.
- Loss of crops, vegetation, and fruits.
- Death of animals.
- Increase in pandemics or diseases.
- Appearance of strange insects.

And regarding corruption in the sea, he defined it as:

- Lack of sea resources.
- Decrease in sea food, fishes, pearls and coral.
- Increase in hurricanes.
- Drying up of the seas and rivers.

Imam Ahmad reported in his *Musnad*: "There was found in the treasure house of Banu Umayyah a grain of wheat the size of a date-stone in a container, on which was written, 'This will grow in times of injustice.'" The meaning of this is that provision will become smaller, more expensive and have less *barakah*.

What is the reason behind all of this? Allah ﷻ tells us in the Qur'an:

Wa-ma asabakum min musibatin fa-bima kasabat aydikum
wa-ya'fu 'an kathir.

"Whatever affliction befalls you is because of what your own hands have committed – and He pardons much." (*al-Shura*, 42: 30)

If Allah ﷻ was not Merciful and He ﷻ did not forgive us as much as He ﷻ does, the afflictions we experience would have been a lot more frequent and a lot worse in severity. Despite this, we shouldn't say to anyone that they are experiencing a difficulty because of what they have done as we have no way of knowing if what they are going through is a form of punishment or a test from Allah ﷻ (as Allah ﷻ also tests those whom He ﷻ loves). Instead, we should focus on ourselves and reflect upon our own actions, discerning if we have been doing anything that could cause an affliction to befall us and those around us.

Sins Withhold Provision

Allah ۞ says in the Qur'an:

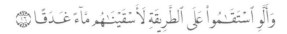

Wa-allawi'staqamu 'ala'l-tariqati la'asqaynahum ma'an ghadaqan.

"Had the deniers followed the Right Way, We would have certainly granted them abundant rain to drink." (*al-Jinn*, 72:16)

When pondering deeply, we come to realise that rain is not just drinking water but also a means to grow other provision, such as crops and vegetation. Following the Right Way is not only praying five times a day, or fasting during Ramadan or dressing modestly – these are the bare minimum acts which we must do to be classed as Muslim. Following the Right Way means to do things for the sake of pleasing Allah ۞, ensuring that our intentions are sincere and that we aren't just doing outwardly actions to show others.

For example, when we attend the *masjid*, we must be conscious that the *masjid* is the house of Allah ۞, and our decisions regarding our dressing and actions should be to please Allah ۞. This is following the Right Path, in the way that Allah ۞ wants us to follow it.

Abu Hurayrah, may Allah be pleased with him, heard a man saying: "The wrongdoer does not harm but himself." Abu Hurayrah turned to him and said: "No, by Allah! The animal dies in their own home from hunger as a result of the injustice done by a wrongdoer!" When we disobey Allah ۞, it affects everything around us and everything that we claim we care about – our children, our spouse, our health and more.

Imam Mujahid said: "When an oppressor is given responsibility, he spreads injustice and evil deeds, so Allah ۞ withholds the rainfall and destroys the crops and the cattle. Because Allah ﷻ does not like mischief."

An oppressor is not only a ruler or a politician, but it can also be anyone with some level of responsibility (for example, a father, mother, brother or sister, a manager in a workplace, etc). If someone has responsibility or authority over others, they are capable of committing injustice and may not be paying attention to their actions. For example, when we treat our children or our siblings differently from one another, this is a form of injustice.

Another ayah that shows us how our sins can cause our provision to be withheld is:

وَضَرَبَ ٱللَّهُ مَثَلًا قَرْيَةً كَانَتْ ءَامِنَةً مُّطْمَئِنَّةً يَأْتِيهَا رِزْقُهَا رَغَدًا مِّن كُلِّ مَكَانٍ فَكَفَرَتْ بِأَنْعُمِ ٱللَّهِ فَأَذَٰقَهَا ٱللَّهُ لِبَاسَ ٱلْجُوعِ وَٱلْخَوْفِ بِمَا كَانُوا۟ يَصْنَعُونَ ﴿١١٢﴾

Wa-daraba'l-lahu mathalan qaryatan kanat aminatan mutma'innatan ya'tiha rizquha raghadan min kulli makanin fakafarat bi-an'umi'l-lahi fa-adhaqaha'l-lahu libasa'l-ju'i wa'l-khawfi bima kanu yasna'un.

"And Allah ﷻ sets forth the example of a society which was safe and at ease, receiving its provision in abundance from all directions. But its people met Allah's favours with ingratitude, so Allah ﷻ made them taste the clutches of hunger and fear for their misdeeds."
(*al-Nahl*, 16: 112)

Allah ﷻ gives this parable as a lesson for all of us until the end of time; any city or any country anywhere in the world could become this example. A place may have peace and plenty of provision, but the people may become ungrateful for the blessings that Allah ﷻ has bestowed on them. This ungratefulness then leads people to experience lack of peace, and increase of fear and hunger.

We should ask ourselves if we are also ungrateful to Allah's ﷻ blessings. We believe in the Oneness of Allah ﷻ, however the *kufr* that is mentioned in the above verse, is referring to not being grateful. So many of us show ingratitude daily by wasting food and drink. For example, we may fill a large glass of water but not drink all of it, or leave a water bottle half-full, yet we won't think about using the remaining water to feed plants. We will either pour it down the sink or throw the bottle away. Showing this kind of ingratitude has consequences, and we are told in the above ayah that these consequences are the feelings of insecurity and hunger.

The cost of living has increased in current times, with staple household or food items becoming more and more expensive. Allah ﷻ is the One who provides, and He is the One who allows things to become expensive. It is important for us to look at our actions and understand that it may be due to them that we are experiencing such difficulties.

I would like to mention here another eye-opening quote from Mujahid, who said: "When rain will be held and droughts appear, the animals will curse the son of Adam and will say, 'This is a result of the sins of the son of Adam!'" This is extremely profound, and we must look at ourselves and our actions. Do we want to be cursed by the animals? When we experience heatwaves and the animals begin to suffer too, we will be cursed by them because they know that we have sinned and brought this hardship upon everyone. However, we should also remember that Allah ﷻ sometimes tests us through hardships and natural disasters or difficulties. Therefore, we should not consider all disasters as punishments.

Sins not only affect our provisions, but they also affect our shape as human beings. We can understand this better with the following Hadith, as narrated by Abu Hurayrah, may Allah ﷻ be pleased with him: "Allah's Messenger ﷺ said: 'Allah, the Exalted and Glorious, created Adam in His image, his height is sixty cubits, and when He created him He said: "Go and greet those people, and they are a group of angels, sit down and listen to what they answer you, for they greet you and greet your descendants." He then went and said: "Peace be upon you," and they said: "Peace be upon you and the mercy of Allah be upon you." They increased and added "mercy of Allah ." So, whoever enters Paradise will be in the form of Adam, his length being sixty cubits. Then the people who followed him continue to diminish in size to this day."' (*Muslim*, 2841) This hadith suggests that the height of people has been and continues to decrease because of their actions. We are forgetting the teachings of Allah and His Messengers and do not act accordingly.

The Prophet Adam, may Allah's peace and blessings be upon him, greeted the angels with *al-salamu 'alaykum*, and Allah made this greeting the greeting of Jannah. However, nowadays we have become too lazy or even embarrassed to greet each other with *al-salamu 'alaykum*. This greeting of *salam* is a *du'a* that we make for each other.

Sins cause Calamities

The following Hadith highlights five things with which we will be tested, whilst also telling us that the punishment for a sin is similar or equal to the sin that has been committed. The Hadith is narrated by Abdullah ibn Umar who said: "The Messenger of Allah turned to us and said: 'O Muhajirun, there are five things with which you will be tested, and I seek refuge with Allah lest you live to see them. Immorality never appears among a people to such an extent that they commit it openly but that plagues and diseases that were never known among the predecessors will spread among them. They do not cheat in weights and measures but that they will be stricken with famine, severe calamity and the oppression of their rulers. They do not withhold the *zakat* of their wealth but that rain will be withheld from the sky, and were it not for the animals, no rain would fall on them. They do not break their covenant with Allah and His Messenger but that Allah will enable their enemies to overpower them and take some of what is in their hands. Unless their leaders rule according to the Book of Allah and seek all good from that which Allah ﷻ has revealed, Allah will cause them to fight one another.'" (*Ibn Majah,* 4019)

The immorality that is mentioned in this Hadith, is referring to intimate relationships outside of marriage. This kind of immorality has become widespread in many societies across the world and is publicly accepted. In addition to this, weighing and measuring unjustly is not only limited to buying and selling, but it also extends to treating others justly. For example, when it comes to our personal rights, we want to be given them all without question, but when it comes to giving others their rights, we look for excuses not to. The consequences of injustice are famine, severe calamity, and oppression at the hands of rulers.

Regarding *zakat*, it is something that we should never, ever overlook. It is one of the five pillars of Islam, and this is something we must accept. *Zakat* is not the same as paying taxes to the government, it is the right of Allah ﷻ, and if we are not fulfilling this right of Allah ﷻ, then we should be prepared to have no rain. Whenever we see rain, not only should we thank Allah ﷻ for this blessing, but we should also be aware that Allah ﷻ is feeding the animals because if there were no animals, then we would undoubtedly experience an extreme lack of rain. The covenant that is being referred to in the above Hadith is the one that we made with Allah ﷻ when we confirmed that He ﷻ is our Lord. Whilst we do still say that Allah ﷻ is our Lord, the question that must be asked is whether we put Allah ﷻ first in our lives. Do we base our actions on pleasing Allah ﷻ first and foremost or do we live our lives through the lens of people and pleasing them as well as our *nafs*? If we do not put Allah ﷻ first, then the consequence that we will bear is being overpowered by the enemies of Islam.

When we or those in charge (rulers) begin to pick and choose what we want to follow from the Qur'an and leave that which doesn't 'suit us' then we will experience fighting and quarrelling amongst each other. This has become the norm in Muslim communities and households; we don't follow and apply the Qur'anic teachings wholly, instead we follow whatever is easy for us.

Umar ibn al-Khattab said the following about consequences of sins: "When the wicked people in the villages will have the upper hand over the righteous ones and when the hypocrites will dominate, villages will soon be destroyed while they are flourishing." This suggests that when sinners or sinning becomes the norm and the hypocrites become leaders, and we will all suffer.

In addition to all of the above, a major consequence of our sins is the occurrence of earthquakes. Imran Ibn Husayn narrated that the Messenger of Allah ﷺ said: "'In this *ummah* there shall be collapsing of the earth, transformation and *qadhf*.' A man among the Muslims said: 'O Messenger of Allah ﷺ! When is that?' He said: 'When singing slave-girls, music and drinking intoxicants spread.'" (*Tirmidhi*, 2212)

The word *qadhf* refers to people accusing one another. And this is described as occurring when females sing and music and drinking alcohol becomes widespread – something we are seeing in abundance right now. Many of us listen to music, knowing full-well that it is prohibited in Islam, and we take it a step further by then buying or listening to music and songs by females.

In another Hadith, Abu Malik Ash'ari narrated that the Prophet Muhammad ﷺ said: "People among my nation will drink wine, calling it by another name, and musical instruments will be played for them and singing girls will sing for them. Allah ﷺ will cause the earth to swallow them up and will turn them into monkeys and pigs." (*Ibn Majah*, 4020)

Although these events did not happen during the life of the Prophet Muhammad ﷺ, he knew that his *ummah* would involve themselves in these actions through revelation from Allah ﷻ. Wine and beer are not simply called wine and beer anymore, and they are definitely not referred to as intoxicants – people refer to them with different and 'fancy' names to make it seem like they are not haram. As indicated in this Hadith, the consequences of these sins are an increase in earthquakes and Allah ﷻ changing the way that people look.

A'ishah, may Allah be pleased with her, also narrated: "The Messenger of Allah said: 'At the end of this *ummah*, there will be collapse, transformation and *qadhf*.' I said: 'O Messenger of Allah! Will they be destroyed while there are also righteous among them?' He said: 'Yes when evil is dominant.'" (*Tirmidhi*, 2185)

If we look around our surroundings now, we will be able to see that evil is very often dominant within our societies. Schools, work and public places are all affected by evil, and these actions have become the norm. If we know that evil is being committed, but do not do anything to prevent it, everyone will suffer from the punishments sent by Allah ﷻ. We must stand up strong, even if we are the only ones that are taking a stance against wrong in our local communities.

Protection

The Prophet Nuh, may the peace and blessings of Allah ﷻ be upon him, said some powerful words to his people:

فَقُلْتُ ٱسْتَغْفِرُوا۟ رَبَّكُمْ إِنَّهُۥ كَانَ غَفَّارًا ۝ يُرْسِلِ ٱلسَّمَآءَ عَلَيْكُم مِّدْرَارًا
۝ وَيُمْدِدْكُم بِأَمْوَٰلٍ وَبَنِينَ وَيَجْعَل لَّكُمْ جَنَّٰتٍ وَيَجْعَل لَّكُمْ أَنْهَٰرًا
۝ مَّا لَكُمْ لَا تَرْجُونَ لِلَّهِ وَقَارًا ۝ وَقَدْ خَلَقَكُمْ أَطْوَارًا ۝

Faqultu'istaghfiru rabbakum innahu kana ghaffaran. Yursi-li'l-sama'a 'alaykum midraran. Wa-yumdidkum bi-amwalin wa- banina wa-yaj'al lakum jannatin wa-yaj'al lakum anharan. Ma-lakum la tarjuna li'l-lahi waqaran. Wa-qad khalaqakum atwaran.

"Saying: 'Seek your Lord's forgiveness, for He is truly Most
Forgiving. He will shower you with abundant rain. And
supply you with wealth and children, and give you gardens
as well as rivers. What is the matter with you that you are
not in awe of the Majesty of Allah? When He truly created
you in stages [of development]?'"
(*Nuh*, 71: 10-14)

The Prophet Nuh was telling his people to ask forgiveness from
Allah ﷻ for their sins. We must also realise our sins and ask for
forgiveness and make the intention to change for the better. If we
keep denying the fact that we sin, we will never be able to change.
And if we are unaware of what we have done wrong, we should ask
Allah ﷻ to show us how we have sinned, just as Umar ibn al-Khattab, may Allah be pleased with him, would ask Allah ﷻ to show him
his shortcomings.

A man once came to the Prophet Muhammad ﷺ and told him: "I
don't feel well!" And the Prophet ﷺ responded to him by saying:
"Ask Allah ﷻ for forgiveness."

Seeking the forgiveness of Allah ﷻ should be a daily practice, as we
don't always know what sins we may have committed. Thankfully,
Allah ﷻ has made it so easy for us to seek His forgiveness; we can
make *istighfar* whilst travelling to work or class, or when we are
doing household chores, or going on a walk, or even when taking
a break and sitting down doing nothing else. We should constantly
seek forgiveness because Allah ﷻ will continuously forgive us, as
is highlighted by the Prophet Nuh's use of the word *al-Ghaffar* to
describe the ever-forgiving nature of Allah ﷻ.

We can also see from the aforementioned verses that the Prophet Nuh asked the people what is wrong with them because they
weren't glorifying and honouring Allah ﷻ in a way that suited
Him. He asked why they couldn't see and appreciate the Majesty of
Allah ﷻ. In the same vein, we may say that we honour Allah ﷻ, but

we should take a step back and analyse whether this is manifested in our actions. When we visit the *masjid*, do we honour Allah ☽ with the way that we speak, dress, and behave? After performing *salah* in the *masjid*, do we sit quietly for a while and do *dhikr* or ask Allah ☽ for forgiveness or we do we start having conversations with everyone around us? Honouring Allah ☽ means to care about what He likes and to please Him above everyone and everything else.

Qatadah ibn Rab'i narrated: "When a funeral passed before the Messenger of Allah ☽, he said: 'He, the one who departed will find relief or the departure of him will bring relief.' They said: 'Apostle of Allah, who is *al-Mustarih* and *al-Mustarah*?' Upon this, he said: 'The believing servant finds relief from the troubles of the world, and in the death of a wicked person, the people, towns, trees and animals find relief.'" (*Muslim*, 950)

Bilal, may Allah be pleased with him, was of the *mustarih* because when he was dying, he was looking forward to meeting the Prophet Muhammad ☽ and the other Companions in Jannah. The *mustarah*, on the other hand, are the unfortunate ones who in passing away give relief to people. We should look at our actions regularly and ensure that we are not harming anyone in any way, otherwise we will be from the same group of people who are not missed or remembered in goodness after leaving this world. When we pass away, the place in which we pray (whether at home or in the *masjid*) will cry for us due to missing us and the place parallel to it in the sky will also cry.

When understanding this Hadith, we come to know that this world is a jail for the believer because of its tests and temptations. A believer will feel choked and like a stranger in this world; they will often be looked down upon or mocked because of their choices (to please Allah ☽). We can go to a shopping mall or a theme park, but we will stand out because of the way we dress. We can be in an educational setting, or work, or anywhere else and be the odd ones out because of the way we choose to speak – by not using foul language or slang. A true believer will be like a stranger in this world. Furthermore, it is important to remember that because Jannah is surrounded by the things that our *nafs* does not like and Jahannam is surrounded by the things that our *nafs* is attracted to, it is more difficult for the believers to live comfortably in this world as they are not giving in to their *nafs*.

If we focus on becoming righteous, maybe animals will stop cursing us, and they will be able to live comfortably without suffering from droughts or famines. And maybe the earthquake that was meant to be very strong will become weaker because of our good intentions and actions. We should not justify sins, neither for ourselves nor for others, but we should gently remind other people of what is right and wrong. We should begin the process of change within ourselves and lead others towards righteous actions by being a good example.

Chapter 7

Sins Affect the Heart

The Messenger of Allah ﷺ said: "Verily, when the slave (of Allah ﷻ) commits a sin, a black spot appears on his heart. When he refrains from it, seeks forgiveness and repents, his heart is polished clean. But if he returns, it increases until it covers his entire heart." (*al-Tirmidhi*)

This final chapter will focus on something that many of us pay little or no attention to: how sins affect the heart. The heart is not just an organ, but it is something very spiritual. Our feelings, emotions and our thoughts are all connected to the spiritual heart. When we praise Allah ﷻ after seeing something beautiful in nature, it is not just our tongue that is moving, rather the tongue is a result of our spiritual heart being connected to and affected by the Majesty of Allah ﷻ.

Just as the physiological heart must be working properly to ensure that blood is pumped to the rest of the body, our spiritual heart must also be well and truly alive if we are to be in a state that allows us to obey and please Allah ﷻ. Both our good deeds and our bad deeds (sins) affect our heart, our relationship with Allah ﷻ, our future actions, our way of living and even our mental health.

Why is it important to care for and pay attention to our spiritual heart? Allah ﷻ mentions in the Qur'an the Prophet Ibrahim, may the peace and blessings of Allah be upon him, as saying:

وَلَا تُخْزِنِي يَوْمَ يُبْعَثُونَ ۝ يَوْمَ لَا يَنفَعُ مَالٌ وَلَا بَنُونَ ۝
إِلَّا مَنْ أَتَى ٱللَّهَ بِقَلْبٍ سَلِيمٍ ۝

*Wa-la tukhzini yawma yub'athun. Yawma la yanfa'u malun
wa-la banun. Illa man ata'l-laha bi-qalbin salim.*

"And do not disgrace me on the Day all will be resurrected
– the Day when neither wealth nor children will be of any
benefit. Only those who come before Allah ﷻ with a pure
heart will be saved." (*al-Shu'ara'*, 26:87-89)

A pure heart will be the only thing that saves us from the Hellfire
on the Day of Judgement.

One of the most beautiful ayāt from the Qur'an related to the
heart reads:

ٱللَّهُ نَزَّلَ أَحْسَنَ ٱلْحَدِيثِ كِتَٰبًا مُّتَشَٰبِهًا مَّثَانِيَ تَقْشَعِرُّ مِنْهُ جُلُودُ ٱلَّذِينَ
يَخْشَوْنَ رَبَّهُمْ ثُمَّ تَلِينُ جُلُودُهُمْ وَقُلُوبُهُمْ إِلَىٰ ذِكْرِ ٱللَّهِ ... ۝

*Allahu nazzala ahsana'l-hadithi kitaban mutashabiham
mathaniya taqsha'irru minhu juludu'l-ladhina yakhshawna
rabbahum thumma talinu juluduhum wa-qulubuhum ila
dhikri'l-lah.*

"It is Allah ﷻ Who has sent down the best message – a
Book of perfect consistency and repeated lessons – which
causes the skin and hearts of those who have awe of (or fear)
their Lord to tremble, then their skin and hearts soften at
the mention of the mercy of Allah ﷻ." (*al-Zumar*, 39:23)

Allah ﷻ describes the hearts of those who are in awe of Him as
trembling and softening after hearing or reading the lessons given
in the Qur'an. Those who are in awe of Allah ﷻ will always be
thinking if their actions are pleasing to Allah ﷻ; they will want to

make sure that everything they say and everything they do is pleasing to their Lord. If we hear or read the Qur'an and it doesn't give us goosebumps or we don't feel emotional, then we should know that our hearts are not softened. Those who have softened hearts will cry – although it may not be every single time – and they will feel a closer connection to Allah ﷻ.

Hardened hearts, on the other hand, remain unaffected by the words of Allah ﷻ and they miss out on the beauty of the *din* and Allah's Message, as described in the following verse:

ثُمَّ قَسَتْ قُلُوبُكُم مِّنْ بَعْدِ ذَٰلِكَ فَهِيَ كَٱلْحِجَارَةِ أَوْ أَشَدُّ قَسْوَةً وَإِنَّ مِنَ ٱلْحِجَارَةِ لَمَا يَتَفَجَّرُ مِنْهُ ٱلْأَنْهَـٰرُ وَإِنَّ مِنْهَا لَمَا يَشَّقَّقُ فَيَخْرُجُ مِنْهُ ٱلْمَآءُ وَإِنَّ مِنْهَا لَمَا يَهْبِطُ مِنْ خَشْيَةِ ٱللَّهِ وَمَا ٱللَّهُ بِغَـٰفِلٍ عَمَّا تَعْمَلُونَ ﴿٧٤﴾

Thumma qasat qulubukum mim ba'di dhalika fahiya ka'l-hijarati aw ashaddu qaswatan, wa- inna mina'l-hijarati lama yatafajjaru minhu'l-anhar. Wa-inna minha lama yashshaqqaqu fayakhruju minhu'l-ma'. Wa-inna minha lama yahbitu min khashyati'l-lahi wa-ma'l-lahu bighafilin 'amma ta'malun.

"Even then your hearts became hardened like a rock or even harder, for some rocks gush rivers, others split, spilling water, while others are humbled in awe of Allah ﷻ. And Allah ﷻ is never unaware of what you do." (*al-Baqarah*, 2:74)

When we disobey Allah ﷻ and we don't feel any remorse, then our hearts have become hardened. When we cannot forgive someone, then our hearts are hardened.

Our hearts also enable us to see; they are like a window from which we can see right and wrong. However, committing sins can lead to weakening the heart's insight and can blind it. When it cannot see properly anymore due to sinning, we are unable to make the correct decisions that will take us towards the Right Path.

Two people could be in the same place at the same time, for example a *masjid*, but one only sees the building as a place to pray, whilst the other sees the *masjid* as a blessing from Allah ﷻ, as a house of Allah ﷻ and as a place to increase worship and to carry out voluntary good deeds. The second person is seeing with their heart and has insight, whilst the first is only seeing with their eyes.

Allah ﷻ describes this insight in *Surah al-Hajj*:

أَفَلَمْ يَسِيرُوا۟ فِى ٱلْأَرْضِ فَتَكُونَ لَهُمْ قُلُوبٌ يَعْقِلُونَ بِهَآ أَوْ ءَاذَانٌ يَسْمَعُونَ بِهَا فَإِنَّهَا لَا تَعْمَى ٱلْأَبْصَٰرُ وَلَٰكِن تَعْمَى ٱلْقُلُوبُ ٱلَّتِى فِى ٱلصُّدُورِ ۝

Afalam yasiru fi'l-ardi fatakuna lahum qulubun ya'qiluna biha aw adhanun yasma'una biha fa-innaha la ta'ma'l-absaru wa-lakin ta'ma'l-qulubu'l-lati fi'l-sudur.

"Have they not travelled throughout the land so their hearts may reason and their ears may listen? Indeed, it is not the eyes that are blind, but it is the hearts in the chests that grow blind." (*al-Hajj*, 22:46)

Here, Allah ﷻ is asking a rhetorical question about people walking and travelling on the earth and not comprehending the signs that surround them. In our daily lives, we could be stuck in traffic, but the way we think in that situation can make us different from everybody else. Most people will just be thinking about how awful or annoying it is to be stuck in traffic or how late they will be. But a person with insight, a person who comprehends things with their heart, may be thinking about how long it will take them to cross the bridge on the Day of Judgement to reach the gates of Jannah. The job of the spiritual heart is to think more deeply - to think about and realise the miracles of Allah ﷻ, our responsibilities as a family member and as a member of the wider community, and to think about how we can utilise the blessings of Allah 🙵 before we are asked about this.

Every time that we obey Allah 🙵, we will be able to see the Truth more clearly. Actions or deeds that start off as difficult, become easier the more we want to obey Allah 🙵.

Surah Qaf very vividly describes what will happen at the time of death and on the Day of Judgement and follows this description with a very profound statement:

إِنَّ فِى ذَٰلِكَ لَذِكْرَىٰ لِمَن كَانَ لَهُۥ قَلْبٌ أَوْ أَلْقَى ٱلسَّمْعَ وَهُوَ شَهِيدٌ ۝

Inna fi dhalika la-dhikra liman kana lahu qalbun aw alqa'l-sam'a wa-huwa shahid.

"Surely this is a reminder for whoever has a mindful heart and lends an attentive ear."   (*Qaf*, 50:37)

Allah 🙵 does not mention the brain but the heart as something that is mindful. Those whose spiritual heart is alive will remember the reality of this life and the Day of Judgement. And in another Hadith, Abu Hurayrah narrated that the Messenger of Allah 🙶 said: "Verily, Allah 🙵 does not look at your bodies or your faces, but He looks to your hearts [and he pointed towards the heart with his fingers]." (*Muslim*, 2564b)

The Messenger of Allah 🙶 also explained to us how the heart is affected by good and bad. Ali ibn Ibrahim narrated from his father, from Ibn Abu Umayr, from Hammad, who narrated that the Prophet 🙶 said: "There is no heart without two ears. On one of them there is an angel who provides guidance and on the other there is a devil who induces temptation. This one commands him and that one prohibits him. The devil commands him to disobey and the angel prohibits from sins as it is mentioned in the words of Allah 🙵, the

Most Majestic, the Most Holy: 'since the two scribes are sitting on each of his shoulders, he does not utter a word that is not recorded immediately by the watchful scribes.' (*Surah Qaf*, 50:17-18)" (*Mir'at al-'Uqul Fi Sharh Akhbar al-Rasul*, 9/377)

Sickness of the Heart

Just as our physical heart can be affected by illness, so too can our spiritual heart by sins. Allah ﷻ even describes this concept in *Surah al-Baqarah*:

Fi qulubihim maradun fa-zadahumu'l-lahu marada.

"There is sickness in their hearts, and Allah only lets their sickness increase." (*al-Baqarah*, 2:10)

Disease or sickness of the heart is very real and something that we cannot deny as Allah ﷻ has mentioned it in the above verse. However, there are two questions that we must ask ourselves regularly:

 – Do we know that we have sickness in our hearts?
 – What are we doing to eliminate that sickness?

Allah ﷻ further mentions in *Surah al-Ma'idah* that those with sickness in their hearts compromise their *din* to please people:

Fa-tara'l-ladhina fi qulubihim maradun yusari'una fihim yaquluna nakhsha an tusibana da'irah.

"So, you see those with disease in their hearts racing into association with them, saying: 'We are afraid a misfortune may strike us.'" (*al-Ma'idah*, 5:52)

Do we worry about what people will say if we do or do not do something? This is something that we must take into consideration. If we are worried about what people will say, rather than worrying about disobeying Allah 🕮 and risking our Hereafter, then indeed we have a major sickness in our hearts.

Having sickness in our hearts can also affect the way we perceive people and what they say. Allah 🕮 gave advice to the wives of the Prophet 🕮 regarding their speech so that they would not be affected by those with sick hearts:

Ya nisa'a'l-nabiyyi lastunna ka-ahadin mina'l-nisa'. In ittaqaytunna fa-la takhda'na bi'l-qawli fayatma'a'l-ladhi fi qalbihi maradun wa-qulna qawlan ma'rufa.

"O wives of the Prophet! You are not like any other women; if you are mindful of Allah 🕮, then do not be soft in speech with men or those with sickness in their hearts, lest they be tempted, but speak in a moderate tone." (*al-Ahzab*, 33:32)

How we perceive people is a sign of the state that our hearts are in. If we think negatively or falsely about them, our hearts are obviously not in the best state.

How can we know, then, if our faith is strong? What are the signs or actions that can confirm that our faith is strong, and our spiritual heart is very much alive and in a positive state? One sign could be waking up for Fajr without the need for an alarm. Another could be fasting on Monday or Thursday without worrying about missing out on a certain food or drink. Our faith is manifested in examples like these, and they are signs of its strength. However, the opposite of this would be not waking up for Fajr (even with an alarm), or looking for excuses not to fast, or saying things that we regret.

When we look at our hearts, we will be able to see our level of faith. And our actions are a result of our faith. The heart is, in other words, the control station or the hard drive, and our body carries out the actions that our hearts want.

We should regularly look at our actions to see the state of our heart and whether we are being hypocritical. This hypocrisy stems from our heart, as Allah ﷻ describes in the following verse:

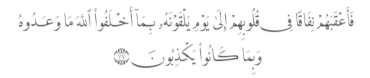

Fa-aʿqabahum nifaqan fi qulubihim ila yawmi yalqawnahu bima akhlafuʾl-laha ma waʿaduhu wa-bima kanu yakdhibun.

"So, He caused hypocrisy to plague their hearts until the Day they will meet Him, for breaking their promise to Allah and for their lies."   (*al-Tawbah*, 9:77)

Allah ﷻ exposed the hypocrites in *Surah al-Tawbah*; the hypocrites were the people who said they believed in the message yet inwardly they disbelieved and could not prove their belief when the time came for them to pledge their allegiance to the Prophet ﷺ. We may also find that on some occasions we promise Allah ﷻ that we will do a certain action or deed if He gives us something, and He gives us what we ask for, yet we don't fulfil our promise. This then results in hypocrisy in the heart.

Doubts are something that also plague the heart. We question why we must do something, even though Allah ﷻ and His Messenger ﷺ have told us to do it. Allah ﷻ mentions in *Surah al-Tawbah*:

إِنَّمَا يَسْتَـْٔذِنُكَ الَّذِينَ لَا يُؤْمِنُونَ بِاللَّهِ وَالْيَوْمِ الْآخِرِ وَارْتَابَتْ قُلُوبُهُمْ فَهُمْ فِى رَيْبِهِمْ يَتَرَدَّدُونَ ۞

*Innama yasta'dhinuka'l-ladhina la yu'minuna bi'l-lahi
wa'l-yawmi'l-akhiri wa'rtabat qulubuhum fahum fi raybihim
yataraddadun.*

"No one would ask for exemption except those who have no
faith in Allah or the Last Day, and whose hearts are in doubt,
so they are torn by their doubts." (*al-Tawbah*, 9:45)

When we start doubting, and we allow these doubts to manifest
themselves in our heart, we look for excuses to disobey Allah ﷻ.
If we really want to please Allah ﷻ, we will prepare ourselves by
genuinely learning and doing actions that are in obedience to
Him. The verse that follows the above-mentioned verse also talks
about preparation the hypocrites would have made had they really
intended to join the Prophet Muhammad ﷺ.

Our doubts can also lead to regrets, and this feeling of regret also
resides in the heart. We begin by doubting or being hesitant about
doing something and because of this, we refrain from doing it, only
to later regret our decision. Allah ﷻ mentions the feeling of regret
and how it causes agony in the heart in the following ayah:

يَٰٓأَيُّهَا ٱلَّذِينَ ءَامَنُوا۟ لَا تَكُونُوا۟ كَٱلَّذِينَ كَفَرُوا۟ وَقَالُوا۟ لِإِخْوَٰنِهِمْ إِذَا
ضَرَبُوا۟ فِى ٱلْأَرْضِ أَوْ كَانُوا۟ غُزًّى لَّوْ كَانُوا۟ عِندَنَا مَا مَاتُوا۟ وَمَا قُتِلُوا۟
لِيَجْعَلَ ٱللَّهُ ذَٰلِكَ حَسْرَةً فِى قُلُوبِهِمْ ۗ ۞

*Ya-ayyuha'l-ladhina amanu la takunu ka'l-ladhina kafaru
wa-qalu li-ikhwanihim idha darabu fi'l-ardi aw kanu ghuz-
zan law kanu 'indana ma matu wa-ma qutilu li-yaj'ala'l-lahu dhalika hasratan fi qulubihim.*

"O believers! Do not be like the unfaithful, who say about
their brothers who travel throughout the land or engage
in battle: 'If they had stayed with us, they would not have
died or been killed.' Allah ﷻ makes that a regret (a cause
of agony) in their hearts." (*Al Imran*, 3:156)

Regrets can cause a lot of uneasiness and unhappiness, and this is all because of the different illnesses affecting our heart. The biggest regret that anyone could have is at the time of death when they ask for more time so that they can change their ways and fulfil the commandments of Allah ﷻ. We can avoid this by preparing for death, and this preparation involves obeying Allah ﷻ and doing what pleases Him so that at the time of death we know that we have tried our best.

Another feeling that stems from the heart is anger. Being treated unfairly or being irritated by someone else's actions can all lead to anger. But when we try our best to control this feeling, Allah ﷻ helps to soothe our heart and remove the anger from it altogether, as mentioned in *Surah al-Tawbah*:

Wa-yashfi sudura qawmin mu'minin. Wa-yudhhib ghayza qulubihim.

"And soothe the hearts of the believers – removing rage from their hearts." (*al-Tawbah*, 9:14-15)

Goodness of the Heart

Good also resides in the heart. We may come across someone we've never met but we want to help them because they need it – this is the goodness in our heart. We feel at peace knowing that we are doing something that will be pleasing to Allah ﷻ, as mentioned in the following ayah:

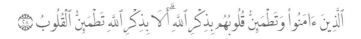

Al-ladhina amanu wa-tatma'innu qulubuhum bi-dhikri'l-la-hi ala bi-dhikri'l-lahi tatma'innu'l- qulub.

"Those who believe and whose hearts find comfort in the remembrance of Allah. Surely in the remembrance of Allah do hearts find comfort." (*al-Ra'd*, 13:28)

The spiritual heart also houses *rahmah* or mercy. Allah ﷻ talks about mercy in the heart towards the end of *Surah al-Hadid*:

$$ ثُمَّ قَفَّيْنَا عَلَىٰٓ ءَاثَـٰرِهِم بِرُسُلِنَا وَقَفَّيْنَا بِعِيسَى ٱبْنِ مَرْيَمَ وَءَاتَيْنَـٰهُ ٱلْإِنجِيلَ وَجَعَلْنَا فِى قُلُوبِ ٱلَّذِينَ ٱتَّبَعُوهُ رَأْفَةً وَرَحْمَةً ... ۝ $$

Thumma qaffayna 'ala atharihim bi-rusulina wa-qaffayna bi-'isa ibni maryama wa-ataynahu'l-injila wa-ja'alna fi qulubi'l-ladhina ittaba'uhu ra'fatan wa-rahmah.

"Then in the footsteps of these prophets, we sent Our messengers, and after them We sent 'Isa, son of Maryam, and granted him the *injil* and instilled compassion and mercy into the hearts of his followers." (*al-Hadid*, 57:27)

When we don't have mercy in our hearts, we should know that our hearts are inflicted with sickness. We need to take care of our heart, and this can only be done by paying attention to what we are doing. Sinning causes us to lose this mercy and will continue to weaken the heart, whilst obeying Allah ﷻ will strengthen the heart and increase mercy and love for others. Love is also a beautiful emotion that is linked to the spiritual heart that Allah ﷻ mentions in the following ayah:

$$ وَأَلَّفَ بَيْنَ قُلُوبِهِمْ لَوْ أَنفَقْتَ مَا فِى ٱلْأَرْضِ جَمِيعًا مَّآ أَلَّفْتَ بَيْنَ قُلُوبِهِمْ وَلَـٰكِنَّ ٱللَّهَ أَلَّفَ بَيْنَهُمْ إِنَّهُۥ عَزِيزٌ حَكِيمٌ ۝ $$

Wa-allafa bayna quluobihim, law anfaqta ma fi'l-ardi jami'an ma allafta bayna qulubihim walakinna'l-laha allafa baynahum, innahu 'azizun hakim.

"He brought their hearts together. Had you spent all the

riches in the earth, you could not have united their hearts, but Allah ﷻ has united them. Indeed, He is Almighty, All-Wise." (*al-Anfal*, 8:63)

The heart is also responsible for being cautious of Allah ﷻ. *Taqwa* is being aware of our actions and remembering Allah ﷻ before we do or say anything (therefore, it influences our actions and allows us to do what is right). Abu Hurayrah reported that the Prophet Muhammad ﷺ said: "*Taqwa* is here [and he pointed to his chest three times]." (Hadith 35, *Forty Hadith of al-Nawawi*)

The Effects of Good and Bad Deeds on the Heart

The mercy of Allah ﷻ conceals the smell of our sins, otherwise if sins were to have a smell, we would not like each other's company. When we sin, our heart begins to be sealed and black spots appear on it. Abu Hurayrah, may Allah be pleased with him, narrated that the Messenger of Allah ﷺ said: "Verily, when the slave of Allah ﷻ commits a sin, a black spot appears on his heart. When he refrains from it, seeks forgiveness and repents, his heart is polished clean. But if he returns, it increases until it covers his entire heart. And that is the '*ran*' which Allah ﷻ mentioned: 'Nay, but their hearts have been stained (*ran*) by all the evil they used to commit!' (*al-Mutaffifin*, 83:14)" (*Tirmidhi*)

Al-Hasan al-Basri said regarding *ran*: "It is one sin on top of another sin, until the heart becomes blind." The heart becomes rotten and blackened by the accumulation of our sins. A big sign that our hearts are being sealed is when someone tells us that something is correct but we see it as wrong or when they tell us that something is not pleasing to Allah ﷻ but we do it anyway because it is pleasing to our *nafs*.

Asking for forgiveness after committing a sin will remove the black stain from our heart and allow us to make amends by doing that which is right. However, if we fail to repent and change our ways, these stains increase on our heart until it reaches the point of being completely sealed.

Committing sins also weaken the determination of the heart, causing our resolve to do a good deed to become weaker whenever we sin. An example of this can be seen in the continuation of our good deeds outside of Ramadan. When Ramadan arrives, we usually have the determination to increase our good deeds, but outside of Ramadan, this determination decreases. We get into the habit of fasting during Ramadan and think to ourselves that we will continue to fast once or twice a week, and we may even do it for a while, but then our determination begins to dwindle as our sins increase and we start giving importance to other desires.

Every time we disobey Allah ﷻ, we become weaker in our intentions and ability to do good deeds, and the strength to disobey Allah ﷻ increases. This also weakens our ability and resolve to seek forgiveness. Repenting is like washing the dirt off the dishes – if we do not wash the dishes, the dirt will increase, harden and settle until it becomes impossible to clean.

On the authority of the son of Abbas, may Allah ﷻ be pleased with them both, the Messenger of Allah ﷺ related the saying from his Lord ﷻ: "Allah has written down the good deeds and the bad ones. Then He explained it [by saying that] he who has intended a good deed and has not done it, Allah ﷻ writes it down with Himself as a full good deed, but if he has intended it and done it, Allah ﷻ writes it down with Himself as from ten good deeds to seven hundred times or many times over. But if he has intended a bad deed and has not done it, Allah ﷻ writes it down with Himself as a full good deed, but if he has intended it and has done it, Allah ﷻ writes it down as one bad deed." (*al-Bukhari and Muslim*)

This Hadith shows the Mercy of Allah ﷻ and how easy He has made it for us to gain rewards through good deeds. It is only through our lack of determination and insistence upon sin that we make it hard for ourselves.

In another Hadith narrated by Anas Ibn Malik, may Allah be pleased with him, the Messenger of Allah ﷺ returned from the *ghazwah* of Tabuk, and when he approached Madinah, he said: "'There are some people in Madinah who were with you all the time, you did not travel any portion of the journey nor cross any valley but they were with you.' The people said: 'O Allah's Messenger ﷺ! Even though they were at Madinah?' He said: 'Yes because they were stopped by a genuine excuse.'" (*al-Bukhari*, 4423)

Not being able to carry something out even though we intended to should not put us down. Instead, we should fully trust that Allah ﷺ knows better than us and did not allow it to happen for whatever reason He knows best and that our good intentions will be written down as good deeds. However, on the other hand, we should not find excuses for committing sins as sins darken the heart. The darkening of the heart stops us from seeing things the way that Allah ﷺ or the Prophet Muhammad told us to see them.

Obeying Allah ﷺ brings light as Allah ﷺ is Light, as is explained in the following verse:

$$۞ ٱللَّهُ نُورُ ٱلسَّمَٰوَٰتِ وَٱلۡأَرۡضِ ۚ مَثَلُ نُورِهِۦ كَمِشۡكَوٰةٍ فِيهَا مِصۡبَاحٌ ۖ ٱلۡمِصۡبَاحُ فِى زُجَاجَةٍ ۖ ٱلزُّجَاجَةُ كَأَنَّهَا كَوۡكَبٌ دُرِّيٌّ يُوقَدُ مِن شَجَرَةٍ مُّبَٰرَكَةٍ زَيۡتُونَةٍ لَّا شَرۡقِيَّةٍ وَلَا غَرۡبِيَّةٍ يَكَادُ زَيۡتُهَا يُضِىٓءُ وَلَوۡ لَمۡ تَمۡسَسۡهُ نَارٌ ۚ نُّورٌ عَلَىٰ نُورٍ ۗ يَهۡدِى ٱللَّهُ لِنُورِهِۦ مَن يَشَآءُ ۚ وَيَضۡرِبُ ٱللَّهُ ٱلۡأَمۡثَٰلَ لِلنَّاسِ ۗ وَٱللَّهُ بِكُلِّ شَىۡءٍ عَلِيمٌ ۝$$

Allahu nuru'l-samawati wa'l-ard. Mathalu nurihi ka-mish-
katin fiha misbah. Al-misbahu fi zujajah. Al-zujajatu
ka-annaha kawkabun durriyyun yuqadu min shajaratin
mubarakatin zaytunatin la sharqiyyatin wa-la gharbiyyatin
yakadu zaytuha yudi'u wa-law lam tamsashu nar. Nurun

'ala nur. Yahdi'l-lahu li-nurihi man yasha'u wa-yadribu'l-la-
hu'l-amthala li'l-nasi wa'l-lahu bi-kulli shay'in 'alim.

"Allah ﷻ is the Light of the Heavens and the Earth.
The example of His light is like a niche within which is
a lamp, the lamp is within glass, the glass as if it were a
pearly white star lit from the oil of a blessed olive tree,
neither of the east nor of the west, whose oil would almost
glow even if untouched by fire. Light upon light! Allah ﷻ
guides to His light whom He wills. And Allah ﷻ presents
examples for the people, and Allah ﷻ is knowing of all
things." (*al-Nur*, 24:35)

When we are unable to see reality for what it is, we need to reignite
the light in our heart, as we were all given this light by Allah ﷻ.
Death is a stark reality that we can be faced with at any time, so
it's vital that we acknowledge and prepare for it. The best form of
light for our hearts is the remembrance of Allah ﷻ. We can incor-
porate remembrance or *dhikr* into our daily routine so easily by saying *alhamdulillah* for the blessings Allah ﷻ gives every day, such as
our eyesight, or being able to eat or dress comfortably, or by saying
subhan Allah when we see Allah's wonders in the form of nature or
even seeing a cute baby.

If we notice that we are not seeing reality the way we should see
it, we need to bring back the light to our heart. We need to keep
working on this light to keep it strong and to keep out the darkness. Abdullah Ibn Abbas, may Allah ﷻ be pleased with him, said:
"The good deeds bring illumination to the face, light to the heart,
more sustenance, strength in the body and the love of people for the
person. Sins bring darkness to the face, darkness in the heart and
the grave, weaknesses in the body, less sustenance and hatred in the
heart of people for the person."

The light on a person's face that appears through their good deeds
is something that is not easily describable. It is something beautiful

and different – something that no amount of skincare or make-up can bring. People will feel love and respect for this person, even if they don't know them very well.

We usually underestimate good deeds, but we should remember that every good deed is valuable. Our good deeds not only bring about light on our faces, but they can also open doors and blessings that we had no expectation of. We may get accepted into university or be offered a job or project that we had no expectation of getting because we didn't meet the standard criteria, but our good deeds pleased Allah ﷻ so He blessed us with success and sustenance. With good deeds, our hearts become purer, lighter and happier. We become content with what we have, even if it may seem less when compared to others.

Obeying Allah ﷻ brings us blessings in so many ways, but disobeying Allah ﷻ takes those blessings away from us. In this case, we may find that people can begin to dislike, hate, or feel uncomfortable around us for no apparent reason. Our face will show no sign of light but will instead exhibit a dullness or darkness to it. We will not be happy with what we have, sustenance might become difficult and no matter what we do in terms of worldly efforts, we see no success. This is notwithstanding the fact that sometimes these could be just tests from Allah ﷻ, and/or medical conditions, like depression.

Disobeying Allah ﷻ and committing sins takes the heart away from its natural state of piety to a state of corruption and deviation. For example, we could be given the opportunity to do a good deed, yet we choose not to. Our sins may have stopped us from doing this good deed, as sins affect the heart just as a disease affects the body. When we suffer from a high fever, we don't find the energy to move our body. Likewise, when our heart becomes weak due to sins, we are unable to obey Allah ﷻ properly.

Protection

The health of our spiritual heart is the biggest investment that we can make in this life. Whilst it is important to put in effort for our families, for our livelihoods and for our community, we must not do it at the expense of making our hearts sick. One very important question we must ask ourselves is where our heart is spiritually. It is something that we need to evaluate regularly because it is the heart that connects to Allah ﷻ, and if this component is weakened, dying or dead, then we will not be able to connect with our Lord.

Imam Ibn al-Qayyim, may Allah be pleased with him, said a very profound statement: "Sin will either kill the heart, or it will make it very sick, or it will weaken it until it is occupied by the eight things that the Messenger of Allah ﷺ sought refuge from." The eight things that the Prophet ﷺ sought refuge from are reported by Anas Ibn Malik, may Allah be pleased with him: "The Prophet ﷺ used to say: 'O Allah ﷻ! I seek refuge with You from worry and grief, from incapacity and laziness, from cowardice and miserliness, from being heavily in debt and from being overpowered by other men.'" (*al-Bukhari*)

Whenever we wake up in the morning, we should make this supplication as per the Sunnah of the Prophet Muhammad ﷺ. When our hearts are sick, they are usually occupied by one of the eight things mentioned in this Hadith. When our hearts are weak, we become unable to do something that we want to do, even though we know it is good and right, or we know that something is wrong, yet we still do it.

Our hearts will suffer from the above-mentioned issues when they are dead or sick, and the only reason they have these issues is because they have become distant from Allah ﷻ through our sins – intentionally or unintentionally.

In order to enjoy the grace of Allah ﷻ in this world and the Here-after, we need to make the intention and put in the effort to stop ourselves from following our desires and obeying the whispers of Shaytan. Allah ﷻ explains:

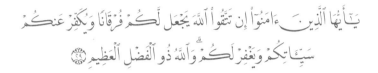

Ya-ayyuha'l-ladhina amanu in tattaqu'l-laha yaj'al lakum furqanan wa-yukaffir 'ankum sayyi'atikum wa-yaghfir lakum. Wa'l-lahu dhul-fadl'l-'azim.

"O believers! If you are mindful of Allah ﷻ, He will grant you a standard to distinguish between right and wrong, remove from you your misdeeds and forgive you. And Allah ﷻ is the Lord of Infinite Bounty."   (*al-Anfal*, 8:29)

When Allah ﷻ says "O believers," we should give our full attention to what follows as it will be an important lesson for us. He ﷻ tells us that if we are mindful of Him, we will be less prone to sinning as we can see right from wrong. Our good deeds, the Qur'an, *salah* and the *masjid* will not be seen as burden but as connections to Allah ﷻ.

If we want to have a clear and healthy spiritual heart, we must want it just as much as we would want to get into a top university or job, or just as much as we would like to have a good spouse and children. We must want our heart to be free of sins and closely connected to Allah ﷻ; our level of 'wanting' can make it easier for us to achieve this through the help of Allah ﷻ.

Let us start the process of change today. Even if it is two extra *rak'ah* of *salah*. We should make the genuine intention to change, so that even if we pass away tomorrow, Allah ﷻ is All-Aware of our intention and this can be a means for our forgiveness and entry to Jannah. Let's help each other to obey Allah ﷻ and not to disobey

Him. We shouldn't find excuses for sins – neither for ourselves nor for others – Shaytan will always try to beautify sins, but we must beautify good deeds.

We will end with a beautiful Hadith *qudsi* that will push us all to make the change today *Insha'aAllah*.

Abu Hurayrah narrated that the Prophet Muhammad said: "Allah 🍃 says: 'I am just as My slave thinks I am (i.e., I am able to do for him what he thinks I can do for him) and I am with him if He remembers Me. If he remembers Me in himself, I too, remember him in Myself. And if he remembers Me in a group of people, I remember him in a group that is better than they. And if he comes hands span nearer to Me, I go one cubit nearer to him. And if he comes one cubit nearer to Me, I go a distance of two outstretched arms nearer to him. And if he comes to Me walking, I go to him running.'" (*al-Bukhari*, 7504)

May Allah 🍃 allow us to change our ways, help us have a sound heart, and increase our love and desire to obey and please Him. *Amin.*

Index

A

Abi'l-Dunya, Ibn, 7, 42
affliction, 63–75
Ahmad, Imam, 3–4, 65
al-Basri, Al-Hasan, 5, 88
al-Basri, al-Hasan, 31
alcohol, 54
al-Darani, Abu Sulayman, 31
al-Hawari, Ahmad ibn Abi, 34
al-Jawzi, Ibn, 32
al-Khattab, Umar ibn, 56, 71, 73
Allah, 1–4, 6, 7, 9, 13, 14–15, 27, 32–33, 38–39, 45, 46, 92. *see also*
 Qur'an
 being cautious of, 88
 blessings of, 67–68, 72, 92
 commandments of, 86
 creations of, 9, 28
 disobeying, 33–34, 42, 92
 displeasing to, 39
 forgiveness, 73
 guidance of, 8, 29
 guidance with, 29
 hope, 51
 knowledge of, 25, 29
 mercy of, 69, 88, 89–90
 relationship with, 5, 40, 54
 remembrance of, 91
 revelation from, 72

right of, 70
worshipping, 43
al-Qayyim, Imam Ibn, 5, 93
al-Qurtubi, Imam, 13–14
al-Shafi'i, Imam, 27, 28
al-Thawri, Sufyan, 7, 34
al-Ward, Abd al-Wahhab ibn, 43
Angels, 51
arguments, 56
arrogance, 52–53

B

backbiting, 33
bad language, 60
behaviour, 6
    and actions, 7
beneficial knowledge, 27
betrayal, 59
bullying, concept of, 53

C

calamities, 69–72
charity, 25
chaste woman, 16
cheating, 33
corruption, 63
    description of, 64
    factors, 63–64
crime, 2

D

Day of Judgement, 80, 81
death, 91
deficiency in worship, 31–34
deprivation of knowledge, 25–30

disobedience, 19
   of Allah, 9
droughts, 74

E

environment, 63
ethnicity, 53
evil, 54, 72

F

famines, 74
fasting, 25, 38, 66
forgiveness, 6, 9, 35, 73, 88–89
fortune tellers, 54

H

Hadiths, 19, 30, 45
health, 31
heart, 77–78
   determination of, 89
   good and bad deeds on, 88–92
   goodness of, 86–88
   hardened, 79
   hypocrisy stems from, 84
   protection, 93–95
   sickness of, 82–86
   spiritual, 80–81, 87, 93
hijab, 38
Hurayrah, Abu, 13, 25, 28, 38, 66, 68, 88

I

Iblis, 49, 50, 53
Ibrahim, Ali ibn, 81
immoral actions, 54

immorality, 6–7, 69, 70
injustice, 14
Islam, 2
    enemies of, 70
    knowledge of, 25
    pillars of, 70
Islamic knowledge, 27

J

Jannah, 25, 50
    companions in, 73–74

K

killings, 2, 16
kinship, 30
knowledge, 30
    of Allah, 25
    beneficial, 27
    deprivation of, 25–30
    of Islam, 25, 27
    of religion, 29
    spreading by sharing, 26–27
    student of, 28

L

learning, 28
love, 87
lying, 33

M

Malik, Anas Ibn, 7, 90, 93
Malik, Imam, 27
masjid, 80, 94
Masud, Abdullah ibn, 16–17
Mayyas, Taysalah ibn, 19–20
mercy, 87

Mujahid, Imam, 66–67
Murrah, Abu, 50
Musa, Abu, 29
Muslims, 1, 7–8, 66. *see also* Islam

O

obligations, 38
orphans, wealth of, 16

P

Paradise, fragrance of, 14
personal rights, 70
physiological heart, 77
practice generosity, 44
praying, 25
Prophet, 28, 29
    companions of, 26
    supplications of, 39
Prophet Adam, 9, 53, 69
Prophet Ibrahim, 77
Prophet Muhammad, 8, 13, 39, 45, 56, 71, 88, 90, 93, 95
Prophet Nuh, 34–35, 72–73
protection, 34–35
provisions, 68
punishments, 5, 13–14, 32–33, 68
    angels of, 45

Q

qadhf, 71
qarin, 62
Qudsi, Hadith, 38
Qur'an, 1–2, 10, 14, 26, 27, 29–31, 39, 45, 55, 56, 60, 78, 94
    messages of, 26
    teachings, 58
    whispering of Shaytan, 52

R

Ramadan, 7, 29–30, 53, 66, 89
relationship
    with Allah, 37–39, 41–42, 46–47, 49, 77
    with Shaytan, 49, 53
religion, 29
responsibility, level of, 67
riba, 16
Rab'i, Qatadah ibn, 73
run away from battlefield, 16

S

Sa'd, Sahl ibn, 26
salah, 38, 94
Salamah, Umm, 5
scoffing, 19
self-accountability, 7–8
self-esteem, 54
Shaytan, 7, 9, 32, 40–44, 49
    arrogance, 52
    aspect of, 51
    category of creation, 50–51
    influence of, 54–55
    tools of, 56
    tricks of, 54–62
    whispering of, 52
    whispers of, 94
shirk, 16
Sinning, 32
sins, 16, 27, 93
    affect the heart, 77–95
    affliction, 63–75
    cause calamities, 69–72
    committing, 3, 89, 90
    consequences of, 71
    definition of, 1–2

description of, 1
protection, 72–75
smallness/insignificance of, 4
spiritual heart by, 82
types of, 16, 20–22
withhold provision, 66–69
slave, 38, 77
smoking drugs, 54
society, negative effects on, 6
sorcery, 16
spiritual heart, 3–4, 80–81, 87, 93
suffering, risk of, 5
Sulayman, Abu, 34
Sunnah, 13, 27
Surah al-Baqarah, 82–84

T

Taymiyyah, Ibn, 14
tazkiyah, 7–8

U

Umar, Abdullah ibn, 6, 69
Umayr, Ibn Abu, 81
ummah, 71–72

W

wealth of orphans, 16
worship, deficiency in, 31–34. *see also* Allah

Z

zakat, 6, 38, 69